Philosophies of Catholic Education

This seminal volume takes an interdisciplinary approach to presenting an authoritative account of contemporary philosophies of Catholic education, intersecting the substantive boundaries of education, religious studies, philosophy, and theology to ultimately re-examine these philosophies and reinvigorate the authentic aspects of the Catholic educational endeavour.

Against the backdrop of an increasingly volatile debate between liberal and conservative values within Catholic educational and theological settings, chapters provide a thorough and judicious blending of historical accuracy with contemporary urgency. Combining a diversity of knowledge and historical account – including discussion on Thomism, Christian existentialism, and ideologically oppositional philosophies – the book argues that philosophies of Catholic education are in a new process of evolution necessary in order to justify the aims and priorities of Catholic education.

This book will be of value to academics, scholars, teachers, and researchers with an interest in Roman Catholicism and the philosophy of education. Those more broadly interested in exploring the intersection between education, philosophy, and religion will also find the volume of use.

James Arthur is Professor Emeritus in the University of Birmingham and Faculty Affiliate of The Human Flourishing Program at Harvard's Institute for Quantitative Social Science, Harvard University, USA.

Philosophies of Catholic Education
Linking Neo-Scholastic Legacies and Contemporary Concerns

James Arthur

LONDON AND NEW YORK

First published 2024
by Routledge
4 Park Square, Milton Park, Abingdon, Oxon OX14 4RN

and by Routledge
605 Third Avenue, New York, NY 10158

Routledge is an imprint of the Taylor & Francis Group, an informa business

© 2024 James Arthur

The right of James Arthur to be identified as author of this work has been asserted in accordance with sections 77 and 78 of the Copyright, Designs and Patents Act 1988.

The Open Access version of this book, available at www.taylorfrancis.com, has been made available under a Creative Commons Attribution-Non Commercial-No Derivatives (CC-BY-NC-ND) 4.0 license.

Any third party material in this book is not included in the OA Creative Commons license, unless indicated otherwise in a credit line to the material. Please direct any permissions enquiries to the original rightsholder.

Trademark notice: Product or corporate names may be trademarks or registered trademarks, and are used only for identification and explanation without intent to infringe.

British Library Cataloguing-in-Publication Data
A catalogue record for this book is available from the British Library

Library of Congress Cataloging-in-Publication Data
A catalog record has been requested for this book

ISBN: 9781032749884 (hbk)
ISBN: 9781032781518 (pbk)
ISBN: 9781003486435 (ebk)

DOI: 10.4324/9781003486435

Typeset in Times New Roman
by KnowledgeWorks Global Ltd.

Contents

Foreword: Reviving Catholic Philosophy of
   Education by John Haldane　　　　　　　　　　*vi*
Acknowledgements　　　　　　　　　　　　　　　*ix*
About the Author　　　　　　　　　　　　　　　　*x*

Introduction　　　　　　　　　　　　　　　　　　　1

1　Towards an Understanding of Philosophies of
　　Catholic Education　　　　　　　　　　　　　　9

2　Charisms, Definitions, and Models of Catholic
　　Education　　　　　　　　　　　　　　　　　　32

3　The Legacy of Thomism in Education　　　　　　55

4　Philosophies and Ideologies of Catholic Education　66

　　Conclusion　　　　　　　　　　　　　　　　　　85

　　References　　　　　　　　　　　　　　　　　　94

　　Index　　　　　　　　　　　　　　　　　　　　*99*

Foreword: Reviving Catholic Philosophy of Education

There was a time, not so long ago, when trainee teachers were required to study foundations of education, the core disciplines in this regard being history, philosophy, psychology, and sociology. The idea was that in studying one or more of these as they related to education, one would not only learn certain methods of study and ideas associated with these disciplines but also be better equipped to place the practice of teaching within a broader and deeper context. One question now often unasked is where did formal education come from and why is it structured in the way that it is? History provides part of the answer to that, as does sociology. Another question is about the conditions and trajectory of learning. Psychology provides its methods and theories in addressing that.

What question about education, then, does philosophy help to answer? In one sense all of them, for if a question about history, psychology, or sociology is pressed far enough with a series of 'whys?' it tends to turn into a philosophical question. But more directly, philosophy of education is concerned with its aims, purposes, and values in the normative sense of specifying what these ought to be, that is what are the proper aims, purposes, and values of education. It is not possible to do that without having an account of human nature.

All education presupposes part of one or another such idea, but without serious analysis, this will be partial and often confused: a bricolage of bits and pieces. Clarity and consistency in thinking about the fundamentals of education are hard enough to achieve and maintain, but they are not enough, for one needs a definite positive conception grounded in an account of what human beings are, what befits their nature, and what constitutes human meaning.

One important source of an account of the human is religion, and the most comprehensive and philosophically sophisticated understanding is that proposed by Catholic Christianity. It draws on four sources: scripture, tradition grounded in the teaching of the apostles and their successors, theological and philosophical reflection, and the experience and practice of Catholic communities. From this can be drawn not only a Catholic philosophy of the proper aims, purposes, and values of education in general but also and more specifically a philosophy of Catholic education.

Of course, these two are related but the second brings in particular religious doctrines, purposes, and practices. In adding specificity, however, these elements do not determine a single philosophy of Catholic education, any more than they do a single philosophy of Catholic art and literature, or of Catholic social life. The questions, then, are what philosophies of Catholic education are available and which may be the best?

In this study, James Arthur does readers a great service in setting out a framework for considering these questions and in making a case for a broadly Thomistic approach, that is one that draws on the account of human beings as rational, social, and spiritual animals inhabiting a natural order permeated by grace and directed towards a supernatural completion. In such a view, the aim of Catholic education is to develop those aspects of human beings with a view to assisting them in their journey to God.

One might think that any philosophy of Catholic education would have that aim and purpose, but James Arthur's study brings out two matters that should be of great concern to anyone committed to the cause of Catholic education. First, and in keeping with broader trends in educational theory and practice, there has, over the last four decades, been among Catholic educators a move away from thinking philosophically about education to viewing it from the point of view of processes, structures, methods, and forms of assessment approached in terms of narrow non-educational purposes, principally economic and increasingly political ones. The ideal of liberal education as promoting inward enrichment, critical reflection, and self-control has given way to a combination of narrow vocationalism and extensive social engineering. Catholic education has not escaped this as the training of teachers has become uniform across all sectors and society is shaped by a toxic blend of consumerism and identity politics.

Second, Catholic thinking about education has become fragmented, shallow, and increasingly vacuous: this in consequence of a decline in knowledge about Catholicism itself and a vastly diminished level of commitment to Catholic faith and moral teaching on the part of those in nominally Catholic colleges and schools: students, teachers, and other staff.

Together, these two trends have brought Catholic education to a point of crisis. It is unlikely that it will survive in its present apparent scale – 'apparent' because in reality Catholic schools have largely de-Catholicised in respect of the teaching of scripture and tradition, in the transmission of Catholic thought and culture, and in the encouragement of Catholic sacramental practice. Managing the decline is not only an unworthy aim especially for those supposed to be committed to the virtues of faith, hope, and charity but also it is a futile one since without reform and renewal steady, erosion will soon give way to rapid collapse, evidence of which is already there.

At this point, it is necessary to rebuild the foundations. That is essentially a philosophical task, hence the value of this book. It explores Catholic philosophies of education and considers the fundamental issue of how

Catholic education should be defined, another way of approaching the issues of aims, purposes, and values. It also explores some of the divergent and diminishing trends in what one might term post-Catholic 'Catholic' philosophy of education and makes the case for developing a new comprehensive account.

More precisely, it argues for integrating an informed understanding of the contemporary situation with the perennial philosophy of the human person as developed by Aquinas and his followers in the Thomistic tradition. If this seems quixotic, it is worth pointing out that something similar might have been said 40 years ago about the suggestion of recovering the place of Thomism within contemporary Catholic thought more generally, but that has happened and is bearing ever more and more varied fruit. Time then for the reform to be adopted in the sphere of Catholic education, and this book is a valuable contribution to that work.

Professor John Haldane,
Professor of Philosophy,
St Andrews University, Scotland

Acknowledgements

This short book was completed during my sabbatical at the Angelicum University in Rome during the first semester in 2023–2024. I have had the good fortune to benefit from extensive comments, questions, and conversations that made a difference. In this, I am deeply grateful to Professor Gerald Grace and to the Rev. Professor Simon Gaine OP. I also am particularly grateful to Professor John Haldane for agreeing to write the Foreword. I want to pay tribute to my excellent students who predominantly came from Africa, Asia, and South America – they taught me a great deal and I am grateful to them for the many insights they afforded me.

About the Author

Professor James Arthur is the former Director and Founder of the Jubilee Centre for Character and Virtues 2012–2023 in the University of Birmingham. James was Head of the School of Education from 2010 to 2015 and Deputy Pro-Vice-Chancellor from 2015 to 2019. He was previously Editor of the British Journal of Educational Studies for ten years and holds numerous honorary titles and Fellowships in the academe, including Honorary Professor at the University of Glasgow and Honorary Research Fellow at the University of Oxford. James was made an Officer of the British Empire by the Queen in 2018 and in 2020 won the internationally prestigious Expanded Reason Award from the Ratzinger Foundation in the Vatican. He has written widely on the relationship between theory and practice in education, particularly the links between character, virtues, citizenship, religion, and education. James chairs the Society for Educational Studies and has served on many governmental education committees as well as the Step Up to Serve Advisory Council chaired by His Royal Highness the Prince of Wales (2013–2020). In 2023, his Centre won the prestigious QS Global Award in Education from 1,200 entries. James advises several international charities, particularly the Kern Family Foundation of which he is a Senior Fellow. James graduated with a master's and doctorate from the University of Oxford. He is currently Professor Emeritus at the University of Birmingham and Faculty Affiliate at Harvard University.

Introduction

The aim of this book is to argue that philosophies of Catholic education are in a new process of evolution, but that they lack completeness. This book aims to ameliorate some conspicuous lacunae in writings about Catholic education and its current relevance. My purpose is to provoke discussion because currently Catholic education comprises an amalgam of philosophies characterised by diversity and eclecticism which has given rise to a set of multifaceted Catholic educational institutions operating different goals and theories of education. The text aims to link the legacy of Neo-Scholastic writings on education with contemporary concerns in Catholic education. More specifically, it asks several questions that drive my provocations, like what does 'Catholic' add to education to make it truly Catholic education? Can we identify which mainstream educational philosophies are most compatible with Catholic education? Since a philosophy of education is essentially a statement of one's beliefs about the purpose of education, how we develop and learn, and what and how we should be taught, it would seem reasonable to assume that Catholic faith and life ought to have a contribution to make. If we claim that education prepares human beings for life, then it follows that we need to have some conception of what the purpose of that life is. Therefore, it might be expected we need a theologically based philosophy of Catholic education to justify the aims and priorities of Catholic education.

How can a philosophy of Catholic education mediate Christ as *lumen gentium* in today's secular Western societies? The danger we face is that in the absence of an explicit Catholic philosophy or theology of education, we may make or accept false philosophies, sometimes unconsciously. The numerous partial theories and views of Catholic education are, arguably, sometimes contradictory of one another in terms of their fundamental assumptions about education. This text will look at the pros and cons of several philosophies of education together with the variety of models and definitions that arise from them. It will engage with important debates and questions concerning the nature and purpose of Catholic education and attempt to clarify terms and understandings to make the conversation about Catholic education more enlightening. I am aware that writing on such a wide-ranging theme as Catholic education presents huge challenges, and thus, this short work cannot pretend

DOI: 10.4324/9781003486435-1

This chapter has been made available under a CC-BY-NC-ND 4.0 license.

to be comprehensive. Yet the hope is that at the end of it, readers will have a better understanding and recognition of what might characterise a philosophy of Catholic education.

It is also important to begin this discussion by recognising that we learn a great deal with little mainstream schooling because our lived experiences teach us and learning by any cultural means is part of a lifelong educational formation. Schools and universities are only one group of means by which we receive an education. Catholic education is not simply concerned with schools and universities because the wider cultural context, the community, families, churches, voluntary organisations, the media, and even political life all educate. This could be called the broad or general sense of education, while the narrow or institutional sense of education is confined to school and university. However, this short book will focus on the latter sense – that is on educational institutions long established by the Church as visible signs of its mission to educate that continue to exist in the context of ongoing secularisation. We also begin by recognising that uncertainty, doubt, and scepticism have become common place in the Church and that there is widespread cultural, social, and economic diversities that challenge, confront, and complicate any attempt to construct an authentic philosophy of Catholic education.

A few Catholic critics continue to bemoan the lack of any well-formulated philosophy or theory in support of Catholic education (Topping, 2015). It is also clear that others find the very idea of a philosophy of Catholic education problematic, an oxymoron in which the noun 'philosophy', with its connotations of inherent criticality and open-endedness, is contradicted by the adjective 'Catholic' with its established doctrines. So, not only is there an enduring problem of the relationship between Catholic faith and human culture but also there are ambiguities in the Catholic consciousness itself that reflect its diverse approaches to education. Ambiguity about the meaning and interpretation of Catholic education is nothing new, but an accusation of inexactness in the meaning of the language of Church documents is (see Whittle, 2015). It may be that there is currently an attempt to adapt Catholic teaching to the demands of modernity and hence revise traditional Catholic education. However, it is not yet clear how viable that attempt is especially with over 220,000 schools comprising 70 million students worldwide.

We begin with some pertinent questions. Do Catholic educational institutions have a philosophy of education? If not, is it worth rehearsing and reviving? Are they like secular schools and universities, only that they add a little here and cut out a little there? Can we adequately articulate what makes Catholic education different? Who could be said to be furthering a Catholic tradition of philosophical thought in education? We ask these questions in the light of the many goals claimed on behalf of Catholic education. As Hancock (2017: 108) notes: '… a school can be open to the world while it works to preserve its identity. Still, we must not be naïve. Ideologies, attitudes, and behaviours that are incompatible with Catholic education exist'.

With the honourable exception of the journal *International Studies in Catholic Education*, we need to recognise that there has in recent times not been a sustained scholarly discussion or articulation of Catholic philosophical principles of education as few have taken up this baton, leading to its general marginalisation. Without a clear understanding of the basic principles of a philosophy of Catholic education, it is difficult to explain how Catholic education is significantly distinct from non-Catholic education. While any philosophy of Catholic education is not monolithic, it can be argued that they will have common features compatible with a Catholic anthropology and theology. The basic tenets of this anthropology and theology are generally misunderstood and fragmented in Catholic schools and universities around the world and the practice of these tenets are sometimes unlike each other. What role should the cultural heritage of a group of people holding the Catholic faith have in shaping the contours of Catholic education especially when Catholicism is compatible with diverse cultural dispositions?

This short book is the product of a course in the philosophy of education that I taught in Rome in the first semester of the 2023–2024 academic year at the Pontifical University of St Thomas Aquinas (known as the Angelicum) and is built on some of the notes for the lectures and seminars delivered during that sabbatical year. The sabbatical year was split between the Angelicum and Harvard University. The main argument of the book is that we need to have a fundamental re-examination of our philosophies of Catholic education since there is little sign that current positions will lead to a comprehensive new philosophy of Catholic education capable of resolving the many conflicts created by the different interpretations of Catholic educational practice. I recognise that within certain limits, controversy about Catholic education is both inevitable and desirable. However, every Catholic educator needs to be aware of their philosophical beliefs, of the alternative beliefs they preclude, and of the bearing of these beliefs on educational theory and practice. We simply need to begin by clarifying the meanings of these beliefs, if only to remove vagueness, confusion, and ambiguity of the terms used. This will provide us with a reassertion of the specifically Catholic and authentic aspects of our educational endeavour. Moreover, we need to bring Catholic educational philosophy into a more critical dialogue with secular traditions of educational thought, especially those rooted in an analytical, reason-centred approach.

A philosophy of Catholic education itself is only part of the solution as philosophy will only help explain or justify some issues; it will not lead us to heaven and cannot replace faith. Nevertheless, the Catholic tradition has consistently endorsed philosophy since it trusts reason which is the main source and tool of philosophical thinking. Analogously, it can trust those educational philosophies that are best supported by reason. The Catholic tradition is rich and varied, but above all, it is a living tradition born out of centuries of experience, study, prayer, and rich cultural heritage. This rich tradition of the Catholic Church helps us to learn and re-appropriate it for the purposes of identifying the essential characteristics of Catholic education. Any diversity of philosophies of Catholic education must be commensurable with Catholic teaching and practice. Therefore, it is important to survey the multiple sources for constructing any philosophy of Catholic education. The three principal sources that we need to critically engage with are Scripture, Tradition, and the teachings of the Catholic Church. We cannot bracket out or put aside these religious facets of Catholic education simply because secular educationalists, in and outside of the Church, view revealed doctrines as unreasonable.

A Preliminary Concern

Many educationists, some of considerable influence, have explicitly excluded Christianity from any general consideration of the aims and purpose of education. For example, Paul Hirst (1974) consistently denied the possibility of constructing a useful relationship between Christian faith and education. Indeed, he went so far as to say that Christianity has no contribution to make to an understanding of education and that it would be illegitimate to apply it in this way. He explained that the very search for a Christian philosophy of education is a 'huge mistake' and that religion must never be allowed to determine or influence public issues. The thrust of Hirst's arguments was towards the irrelevancy of religious beliefs, especially dogmatic Catholicism, for an understanding of education. Modern Catholic education has been partially influenced by these views and often reflects a fusion of diverse philosophical thinking and action. Sean Whittle (2015), for example, employing Hirst's philosophy, rules out evangelisation and catechesis in Catholic schools preferring what he terms 'fluidly faithful to Catholicism'. In being critical of what he rightly calls the lack of clarity on Catholic education and 'vague slogan-like descriptors' found in Vatican documents on education, he proceeds to talk about a theology of mystery that equally lacks clarity. Catechesis is essential to Catholic education because the Church seeks to educate better Catholics who believe in Christ and develop a holy life. Evangelisation is necessary too as we seek to help students learn about the Christian tradition either through re-evangelisation or by pre-evangelisation when students learn about and appreciate the Christian tradition. As integral parts of the Catholic Church, Catholic educational institutions must be confident about transmitting the faith especially when they are open to all.

I was taught philosophy of education by Dr John Wilson (1979) at Oxford University in the late 1980s, a well-recognised figure in the philosophy of education community at the time. He taught me to be rather sceptical as he believed that many modern philosophies suffered from a lack of coherence. I see the same problem with the thinking on philosophies of Catholic education today. One of the primary functions of philosophy of education is to help identify and correct conceptual confusion. This is especially important since many new trends in the philosophy of education have sprung up since the 1950s and 1960s

Introduction 5

which have their background in the 20th century. A series of 'ism' movements has represented these trends, and they have impacted upon Catholic education. In addition, various authors have understood philosophy of education differently. In the case of Catholic education, we need to explore how, and if, these different strands and perspectives cohere together. I also attended several classes of Professor Richard Pring (1968: 98–146) while in Oxford, and he was the first Catholic who attempted to apply the methods and philosophical analysis developed by the pioneer of modern educational philosophy in the UK, R. S. Peters, to the ideals and processes of Catholic education. In a book, *Catholic Education in a Secular Society*, edited by Bernard Tucker and published in 1968, he contributed an article entitled 'Has education an aim?' (1968: 98–146). It is interesting that both Pring and Tucker trained for the Roman Catholic priesthood but left before ordination. Tucker's collection of articles was clearly a radical departure from previous Catholic thinking on education since it found the whole justification for a separate Catholic school system questionable. Tucker admits, however, that this was a 'minority view' within the Church.

Influenced by his doctoral supervisor, R. S. Peters, Pring stated that Church education cannot attach meaning to a system issuing from a 'discovered aim' of education, whether the source is religious or not. He does recognise later in the article that the relationship between revelation and education needs to be studied in greater depth. However, despite his aim to clarify education, his chapter does not explicate the meaning of the educational terms used by the Church nor does it examine their conceptual basis. He calls on the Church to accept the basic framework of language and ideas which informs the current debate about education. He sees the value of what the Church has to offer as being understood and justified within the scheme of ideas and values which underpin the whole secular educational system. How the Church could possibly contribute to such a scheme of things remains obscure, especially as Pring (1968: 126) himself states that the Church speaks a 'different language' which is 'ludicrous to many in and outside the Church'. Pring, at this stage, adopted the language of analytical philosophy and viewed education as human-centred and concerned with the development of human potentialities. Education's main fruit is a spirit of criticism which accepts nothing as being beyond questioning. For Pring, education is an initiation into certain ways of thinking and conceptualising, and he concludes that this is the only tenable analysis of what education really is (see Arthur, 1995: 74).

He makes it clear that

> To propose an education programme of which the first principles are a privileged revelation of the Church, (and thus outside rational questioning), and the details of which are simply a question of logical deduction, (and thus necessary truths not open to dispute), is tantamount to the suppression of healthy criticism of the basic principles underlying educational decisions.

Consequently, for Catholic education to be acceptable, in Pring's view, it may need to suppress the importance of the 'revelation' element. Pring's principal point concerns the question of truth which is also central to the Church's view of education. He (1968: 100) finds that:

> Since truth is concerned with what is the case and with the reasons and evidence for believing that something is the case, the role of authority would seem confined to the limited function of initiating the pupil into the adult world of rational enquiry. Anything else could not be counted as education where matters of truth are concerned.

He adds: 'the Church often seems like an alien body in a world which assumes, almost as an axiom, the relativity of truth'. Pring's main philosophical point in this chapter is that the aims of education cannot be discovered or deduced from theological premises. The Catholic Church teaches that the aims of education are partially deduced as a practical consequence of what it means to be fully human in the light of Christ's revelation. Pring has significantly changed his position on these early comments, but he was speaking for or represented the minority view among Catholic academics in the 1960s. Today, he accepts that Catholic education is just as concerned with argument, conceptual analysis, and rigour as mainstream analytical philosophy of education was in the 1960–1980s, before its postmodern turn. The fact that he no longer identifies with these early views can be evidenced in his 2018 publication on *The Future of Publicly Funded Faith Schools: A Critical Perspective*.

Nevertheless, since the 1960s, the perception of Catholic education has become increasingly fragmented, and writings on Vatican II have generated many interpretative difficulties. Indoctrination and sectarianism are accusations that are often levelled against the Church by both those in and outside of the Church, but this is simply a way to try to prescribe Catholic educational practices. Commitment based on convictions and a strong Catholic identity do not close your mind, especially as Catholicism provides wide scope for the exercise of reason. Each student maintains the right to choose and is capable of this as can be seen by the variety of perspectives Catholic students hold. They maintain an ability to think even if exposed to religious ideas, which they clearly do not always accept in their entirety. Catholic education can have a strong identity as a place of catechesis, evangelisation, integral education, mission, and Catholic formation even if all these categories are seen as contentious and controversial. One of the difficulties today in using these terms is with the language and definitions employed, as they are often used in a way that lack clarity and sometimes have contradictory meaning. We need to be careful that the practice of Catholic education does not produce other practices that seek justification on different and incompatible lines of thought. These opposing views may not be in keeping with a Catholic understanding of reality and would constitute an inherent contradiction if used in a Catholic context. The last 30 years have also witnessed the disintegration of the analytical tradition of educational philosophy, spearheaded by figures such as Peters and Hirst, so the fragmentation in education referred to above is not just confined to the tenets of Catholic education.

I argue that we need to forge a link between the Neo-Scholastic legacy and current concerns in Catholic education and philosophy. I suggest that Thomism or Neo-Thomism is open to a more positive appraisal and therefore may help us in re-thinking a philosophy of Catholic education. This is not a retrograde move or a mindless return to some past tradition. Thomas Aquinas always sought the best evidence and listened to opposing thinkers before concluding. There is no conflict in being Catholic and engaging in philosophy based on rational principles because the Catholic philosophical tradition is about rational enquiry. The question of faith and reason converging in one truth is, indeed, the central preoccupation of Catholic educational thinking. Contemporary philosophy of education has a multiplicity of conflicting philosophical paradigms of education which may add versatility to discussions, but these conflicts are often irresolvable. The situation in Catholic educational philosophy today is that the Church seeks openness to dialogue and is tolerant with a multiplicity of positions. It also respects differences between cultures while trying simultaneously to evangelise.

However, Christian evangelisation is banned in majority-Muslim countries and heavily restricted in many others such as China and India. The Church also may underestimate the fact that the impulse behind many secular educational philosophies is to assert a kind of 'mental freedom', rooted in radical post-Enlightenment ideals of authenticity and autonomy, over and against all dogma, especially religious dogma. As James Schall (2008: 32) notes,

> Philosophy is not wisdom, but it is the love of wisdom. It is all right if the same questions are asked again and again until the philosophers explain to the common man exactly the terms of the issue. The philosophical vocation does not mean that philosophers have all the answers, but it does mean it is open to answers from whatever source. It does mean that some things are not true and can be dangerous.

I do not wish to suggest that we ought to remain exclusively within the confines of one single theoretical frame although it is hard to write this without seeming to do that. 'Exclusivism' in the modern Catholic mind is often met with a certain repugnance, and it is not what I would call Catholic to be totally exclusive in education, but are there limits to 'inclusivism'?

One need not venture far into educational, theological, and philosophical discourse about 'Catholic education' to get the sense that often the term is not defined clearly. Educationalists, philosophers, and theologians use the word to pick out any of several views dealing with tension between commitments to faith, reason, context, and tradition. This may lead some readers to wonder whether the term can be used universally with any accuracy. Yet many uses of 'Catholic education' in academic discourse draw upon a vague idea in establishing the category of classification. Because of this lack of clarity, developing a philosophy of Catholic education is liable to create further philosophical problems that are perhaps irresolvable. Since talk of Catholic identity has become a matter of controversy, this text agrees with Archbishop Comensoli's (2019) view that

> The idea of Catholic schooling today and tomorrow requires more than finding ways of combining ideas around the words "Catholic" and "school". We need to get used to thinking of a Catholic school as the compound noun it is meant to be. We need to think of how we can school people in a Catholic way; out of a Catholic perspective; from within a Catholic worldview.

Overview

Chapter 1 describes the background to the current debates on Catholic education and introduces an anthropology of Catholic education. Chapter 2 looks at the different charisms, definitions, and models of contemporary Catholic education. Chapter 3 introduces and traces the scholastic approach and legacy as taught by Thomas Aquinas and his various disciples. Chapter 4 looks at some of the philosophies of education that may be compatible with a philosophy of Catholic education as well as examining some of the philosophies of education that sit in opposition to Catholic education, and finally, a brief conclusion is offered.

1 Towards an Understanding of Philosophies of Catholic Education

There is a widespread belief among teachers and academics that philosophy is much more profound in its concern for theoretical discussion than any concern it may have for its application and relevance to practice. This matches the corresponding belief that philosophy has no practical value. Catholic philosophical thinking, like philosophical thinking in general, has been troubled and weakened in its inclination to close theory off from practice often to save it from the untidiness of human existence. Philosophers – be they secular or religious – often use complicated language which makes the problem thornier (see Ellis, 2001: 27). It is frequently said that theory without practice leads to unrealistic goals, and action without philosophical reflection leads to mindless activism. By engaging in philosophical reflection, we can help clarify what we intend to do and help justify why we do it in a logical and systematic way. Philosophy as a tool examines, synthesises, analyses, speculates, prescribes, and evaluates. It can provide us with nuanced categories, definitions, schemas, and distinctions and offers the possibility of a framework on which to base our notions of what we count as education. It can help us clarify concepts, provide justifications, and ask questions about the nature of knowledge. We can look at the significance of philosophers and thinkers and ask broader questions about social justice and discuss and clarify educational policies.

Philosophy of education is a branch of practical philosophy which concerns the aims and nature of education. It addresses philosophical issues which arise from educational theory and practice. Philosophy of education is simply philosophy about education. It was once commonly taught in schools of education, rather than philosophy departments. Like other theoretical subjects, it has been undermined by the increasingly practical and instrumental focus of teacher education. However, where it still exists, it uses the methods of philosophy to address themes in education. There are many kinds of philosophy, many philosophies, and many ways of philosophising, so there are many kinds of educational philosophy and ways of doing it. Philosophy of education is therefore characterised by a broad theoretical eclecticism. As a discipline, it is essentially secular in orientation and seeks no unified point of view. There is usually an acceptance of pluralism and the diversity

DOI: 10.4324/9781003486435-2

This chapter has been made available under a CC-BY-NC-ND 4.0 license.

of philosophic viewpoints, but not always. It offers us the possibility of a vocabulary and concepts that can serve to advance arguments about education.

Philosophies are theories or attitudes that act as a guiding principle for action. They include values, outlooks, arguments, thoughts, views, conceptions, or opinions and can be formed and operated with or without the help of professional philosophers of education. Contemporary philosophies of Catholic education, as practised in countless settings, are generally pluralist and include a multiplicity of exclusive traditions, trends, and individual positions. It is why philosophical positions have multiplied in the course of recent history and why Catholic philosophers do philosophy within several different perspectives. Many Catholic educators can find it difficult to free themselves from all the educational positions current in society, in which they are so immersed, particularly when the Church rejects some of these philosophies. What count as philosophies of Catholic education? Can we name them? Can rational reflection eliminate the pluralism of competing perspectives? This is unlikely since disagreements that appear in the Church reappear among Catholic philosophers of education.

If you think of the philosophy of Catholic education being one single dynamic continuum with all positions on that continuum being recognised as Catholic education, then this appears to be the settled view, at least officially. This continuum incorporates continuity and discontinuity with Catholic tradition. At one end there is a contemporary progressive position, sometimes called an 'open' position, while at the other end there is a traditional orthodox position, often referred to as a 'closed' position. The names for both ends are usually used in a pejorative sense by those in the opposing camps – one as a 'ghetto mentality' the other seen as 'surrendering to the secular'. They are also polarising terms as they suggest one is authentically Catholic and the other not. But this can also stem from an attitude of 'We are all Catholics, so what does it matter if we believe different things'. It is officially accepted that the diversity of Catholic positions on education can be characterised by one or a combination of features representing the continuity of a philosophy of Catholic education across varying contexts but allowing manifestations of this philosophy to differ. However, surely there must be constants in Catholic education, not least that the goals must align with the mission of the Church.

There is also the Catholic tradition and the teaching of the Church in the form of a set of propositions as to the foundations in faith, mission, and identity of what the Catholic institution should be. The philosophical approach that is currently in operation could be called an eclectic philosophy – an amalgamation of diverse philosophies which attempts to pull together viewpoints from disparate philosophies into a comprehensive whole. This eclectic philosophy of Catholic education suggests an open non-dogmatic and non-systematic form of philosophy, but it often results in little concern for the coherence of the resulting whole. However, there are two aspects to this approach. The first seeks coherence and consistency and places limits and boundaries on what can be selected from diverse philosophies. The second chooses indiscriminately from diverse philosophies assuming that almost anything can be subsumable under the heading 'Catholic' if it coheres minimally with Church doctrines. It can intimate the coexistence of conflicting doctrines as if there were no conflict. As Hans Urs Balthasar (1985: 17) concludes, 'the present situation is characterized by a strong *polarization* in the Church, so much so that a dialogue between "progressives" and "traditionalists" succeeds only rarely'.

The existence of conflicting philosophies of education with Catholicism is nothing new. Jean-Jacques Rousseau, for example, clearly believed in the innate perfectibility of human beings and that the development of human character should follow nature, a nature that rejected the importance of the supernatural. He certainly laid the groundwork for progressive education. His philosophy of naturalism in education is best described in his work *Emile*. Education in this reading was to respect and develop the child's subjective *self*. John Dewey believed that people are motivated by their own utility for themselves and that they are interested in what is useful and relevant. He believed that education is best conducted in a democratic environment free from absolutes that prevent free enquiry. For him, thinking and acting were not separable, thinking was incomplete until tested in experience. In fact, the end of education for John Dewey was human growth – education had no end beyond growth, or to having more and more rewarding experiences. Dewey dismissed the spiritual dimension of the human person because it could not be proved empirically. Essentially, Dewey emphasised experience, activity, and problem-solving in education – not too dissimilar to what Thomas Aquinas advocated 800 years before since Aquinas saw that students are rationally curious and therefore education should give opportunities for problem-solving and critical enquiry. Dewey was not the first to think along these lines. However, he exaggerated the hypothetical-deductive nature of experiential education in his early work.

Philosophy of Education in the 19th century was originally defined around canonical works on education and most learned people would have normally read the works of the 'Great Educators' such as Plato, Aristotle, Augustine, Aquinas, Comenius, Locke, Wollstonecraft, and Rousseau. Two Scots, the first, George Jardine, a professor of philosophy at Glasgow University, and the other, James Gall, Edinburgh clergyman, and writer, wrote the first modern works on the philosophy of education, as philosophy, with *Outlines of Philosophical Education* in 1818 and *A Practical Enquiry into a Philosophy of Education* in 1840. Both books were about the philosophy of teaching. An Englishmen, Thomas Tate, in 1857 wrote a book for training teachers that was simply titled *Philosophy of Education* but had little impact at the time. Tate was self-taught and not a trained philosopher, but it was a time when those with an interest in the philosophy of education could share their views in publications.

By the 1930s and 1940s, a version of John Dewey's educational philosophy began to dominate educational thinking in the English-speaking world. This version was his philosophy of progressive pragmatism which became the reigning dogma in the education profession. The first chair in Philosophy of Education in the UK was held by Louis Amaud Reid in 1947 at the Institute of Education, University of London. There was no universally agreed field, subject matter, or method in the philosophy of education at this time. R. S. Peters succeeded Reid and with his *Ethics and Education* in 1966, he began to change the landscape in the philosophy of education. Peters introduced a new and influential analytical philosophy of education that became dominant, and which essentially saw educational philosophy as a tool for clarifying concepts. Peters was a respected mainstream philosopher with close connections to the leading U.K. philosophers of that time. Peters claimed that philosophers of education should not make normative judgements about educational content or strategies but insisted education was an initiation into worthwhile activities, a claim which introduces a normative aspect and therefore seems inconsistent with his first statement. 'Worthwhile activities' has a prescriptive inclination about it. Yet Peters continued to believe that his analytical philosophy was neutral regarding most practical issues in education, and this came under serious and early criticism (Haack, 1976).

Essentially, the analytical philosophy (sometimes referred to as 'ordinary-language philosophy') of the 1960s–1980s asked three questions: (1) what do you mean? (2) How do you know? and (3) What are your assumptions? In this way philosophy is seen as method or approach rather than a body of knowledge or product to be studied. It is concerned with philosophical reflection and with meaning, with justification, and with examination of assumptions (see Hamm, 1989: 10). It placed little value in the history of philosophy, for instance statements by thinkers such as Rousseau on education. It also ignored positions taken by philosophers on several issues as well as completely ignoring religion. Analytic philosophy refused to develop philosophical theories of education in the standard historical sense, as pursued by thinkers like Dewey. In its heyday, the 1960s and 1980s, it dominated discussions in education because it claimed to root out ambiguity in education. However, it tended to ignore context and applied logic without judgement, form without content.

Despite their methodological and epistemological differences, both Dewey and Peters were first-rate philosophers who took an interest in education, but their educational philosophies, within a short space of time, fell into decline, to be replaced by a series of radical philosophies of education including Marxist, critical theorist, feminist, postmodernist, and Foucauldian perspectives – all of these radical philosophies are, in different ways, antagonistic to Catholicism and interestingly are dominated by the sort of moralistic claims that Peters wanted to eschew. They are all inescapably prescriptive, explaining how education ought to proceed, what it should be for and whose interests it should serve. These philosophies of education are related to power in education and

Towards an Understanding of Philosophies of Catholic Education 13

are therefore concerned with social/political theories in educational practice. Rather than being understood as a sub-branch of mainstream philosophy, as Peters apprehended education, these new philosophies consider the field of educational philosophy to be a subfield of social theory. Education is thus only seen as valuable when it addresses issues of social change. These ideas still epitomise the thinking of many philosophers of education today. Nevertheless, the academic successors of Peters, such as David Carr and John White in the UK and Harry Brighouse in the USA, keep the analytical baton aloft.

Today educational philosophy, as a field, is in decline, especially as part of the preparation of teachers. Bureaucratic prescriptions of what constitutes education are now commonplace caused by frequent legislation and regulations that combine to see philosophy as largely irrelevant. In addition, despite the diversity of philosophies in education, the dominant philosophies in the culture of education can be characterised as subjective, relativist, instrumental, and characterised by a lens of no objective truth since one person's truth is as good as another. What is wrong for one person may be right for another. Instead of a strong sense of human community in education, individualism, competition, and consumption have taken over modern education. This is ironic because most of the dominant theories of educational philosophy nowadays see themselves as strongly anti-capitalist and are often intimately concerned with social justice. Unless the Church pursues a Catholic theology and philosophy of education, we are likely to follow whatever the current dominant philosophy is in society. Can we dialogue and learn from these philosophies – do they help with Catholic identity, stability, and continuity in education?

I would say that the current practice of Catholic education is informed by a fusion of knowledge and ideas from a variety of philosophical sources which attempts to combine all good ideas. Catholic educational practice does not hold rigidly to a single paradigm or set of assumptions. Therefore, it selects different practices from different systems of thought without adopting the full philosophy so that various philosophies of education become integral parts of contemporary Catholic practice. This appears both arbitrary and inconsistent and risks a fundamental incoherence. Indeed, to be philosophical in today's intellectual climate is difficult. There must be limits to this eclectic approach.

Today the Church calls for clearer awareness and consistency of the Catholic identity of the Church's educational institutions all over the world. It seeks to hold identity and inclusiveness together, but this must entail living the Catholic faith differently in different cultural contexts, making for a plurality of identities. Pope Francis (2020) has initiated the Global Compact for Education with seven commitments:

1 To make human persons the centre of education
2 To listen to the voice of children and young people
3 To encourage the full participation of girls and women

4 To see in the family the first and essential place in education
5 To welcome and accept the marginalised and most vulnerable
6 To find ways of understanding the economy and politics
7 To safeguard and cultivate our common home

These seven principles are inspired by the encyclicals of Pope Francis. The reality is that identity emanates from different perceptions about how Catholics understand the mission of Christ. The Pope does not want Catholicism to be closed in on itself and he warns against 'backwardism'. However, this global compact is intended as an alliance between the world's religions, international organisations, and humanitarian groups and therefore the focus is on humanity progressing through education. This compact was not meant to be a discrete Catholic philosophy of education. The Vatican's new Dicastery for Education and Culture effectively seeks a language in education that is effective in communicating with educators, including parents, while at the same time encouraging positive reactions to proposals for action that it makes. It wishes to convey the Church's ideas on education that are easily recognisable and are in understandable Catholic forms. These ideas will need, in the future, to be sufficiently general as to promote wide applicability and appeal, without appearing to threaten too much current interpretations of the purposes of Catholic education understood differently by Catholic institutions and educators. This is a challenging task and will no doubt result in an increasing plurality of philosophies of Catholic education or as the Vatican education authorities now calls it 'a polyphony of movements'.

A normative philosophy of education, such as the Catholic perspective, may propose views about what education should be, what dispositions it should cultivate, why it ought to cultivate them, how and in whom it should do so, and what forms it should take. Redden and Ryan (1942: 3) began their major work, *A Catholic Philosophy of Education*, by observing that 'Modern educational thought and practice are characterized by confusion and bewilderment'. More than 80 years later many would agree that this statement still stands as we witness a striking diversity of views by Catholics about education. How do Catholics recognise the various philosophies of education and identify curricula and teaching methods in their relationship to philosophical positions?

Terence McLaughlin (2002), in *A Catholic Perspective on Education*, observed that it was not obvious that there could be a Catholic perspective on education if by this we mean a single, general, clear, and substantive philosophy. He wrote that in a sense there is no such thing as the Catholic philosophy of education, but rather there are philosophies of Catholic education. And yet an English bishop, Michael Campbell (Whittle, 2017: 173) commenting on his own diocesan schools, confidently wrote that 'The Catholic Church has evolved its own distinctive philosophy of education', but he fails to tell us what this philosophy is or where to find it leaving us with the impression that it is merely an assumption. Of course, he means by this assumption that a philosophy of Catholic education is bred on premises from the Catholic faith that are to be found in Scripture, tradition, and Church teaching. However, a full-blown theory of education needs to be more than just a combination of those three elements. Bishop Campbell in another letter wrote:

> Is it right or sustainable to expect our Mass-going population of 21,000 to support our schools and colleges in which often most pupils, and sometimes teachers, are not practising Catholics? Is it time for us to admit that we can no longer maintain schools that are Catholic in name only?

How would we decide whether a Catholic school is Catholic in name only? There is no official status given to this phrase – 'in name only'.

The Vatican's Congregation for Catholic Education, the predecessor the new Dicastery of Education and Culture, has since the 1970s encouraged openness to alternative philosophical views allowing the phrase, 'Catholic education' to own a more expansive meaning. The documents overall permit multiple readings of what Catholic education might mean in different contexts and there appears to be no authoritative position. There is a need to present a more compelling vision of the future of Catholic education and interestingly it cannot be said that the Vatican simply relies on hierarchical authority in issuing education documents since lay expertise is constantly sought. This brings a powerful confirmation that the non-ordained do share in the educational mission of the Church by their baptism. The Vatican's statements of 'guidance' have also come to rely on theology, and D'Souza (1996: 16) has argued that this reliance on theology for a defence of Catholic education is unconvincing and proposes that we need to acknowledge more clearly education's philosophical distinctions. He states, 'It is the philosophy of Catholic education that enables a theology of Catholic education to secure the appropriate means and ends for the education of the human person – the student'. It is the case that many of these guidance documents bring together any number of different strands that often fail to present a coherent case.

The Congregation for Catholic Education (1982) observed that:

> Certain elements will be characteristic of a Catholic school. But these can be expressed in a variety of ways; often enough, the concrete expression will correspond to the specific charism of the religious institutions that founded the school and continues to direct it. Whatever be its origin – diocesan, religious or lay – each Catholic school can preserve its own specific character, spelled out in educational philosophy, rationale or in its own strategy.
>
> (par. 39)

The Congregation is making it clear that every Catholic institution can have a distinctive identity or religious charism or even a philosophy of Catholic education. In this way, they may choose to emphasise some Christian values over others in their mission. What therefore are the essential characteristics of Catholic schooling? It is possible for a religious charism to become disconnected from the larger Catholic vision when a school seeks to become unique in a way that loses sight of its common mission. The full list of resources and guidance statements from the Congregation for Catholic Education are:

Declaration on Christian Education 1965 (*Gravissimum Educationis*) Vatican Council II
On Evangelization in the Modern World 1975 (*Evangelii Nuntiandi*) Pope Saint Paul VI
The Catholic School 1977
Lay Catholics in School: Witnesses to Faith 1982
The Religious Dimension of Education in a Catholic School: Guidelines for Renewal and Reflection 1982
The Catholic School on the Threshold of the Third Millennium 1997
Catechism of the Catholic Church 2000 (CCC) 2nd edition *Libreria Editrice Vaticana*
Consecrated Persons and their Mission in Schools: Reflections and Guidelines 2003
Educating Together in Catholic Schools: A Shared Mission between Consecrated Persons and the Lay Faithful 2007
Educating to Intercultural Dialogue in Catholic Schools 2013
The Joy of the Gospel 2013 (*Evangelii Gaudiam*) Pope Francis
Educating to Fraternal Humanism 2017
Instruction: The Identity of the Catholic School for a Culture of Dialogue 2022

The Congregation's 2022 publication, an 'Instruction' called *The Identity of the Catholic School for a Culture of Dialogue*, opens with the admission that the Congregation has been confronted with many cases of 'conflict and appeals resulting from different interpretations of the traditional concept of Catholic identity by Catholic institutions'. The document also acknowledges that there are divergent interpretations of the term 'Catholic' in general. Previous documents by the Congregation had also emphasised the vital importance of 'Catholic identity' in education. The Catholic School on the Threshold of the Third Millennium in 1997, for example, saw identity being 'at the heart' of Catholic education and that the Catholic school is 'a place of ecclesial experience' and part of the Church's evangelising mission. Collectively, previous documents outlined the sacramental, ecclesiastical, and catechetical dimensions of Catholic education as well as the educational.

The recent 'Instruction' restates existing Church teaching on Catholic education, but there is a firm commitment to 'Catholic Identity'. While each Catholic educational institution is to develop its own statement of mission, based on Church documents and under the local bishop, it is stated that any institution that calls itself Catholic should be 'Catholic'. Catholic schools must be 'endowed with a specific identity' ... 'centred on Jesus Christ' and uphold and teach the truths of the Catholic faith. It states that 'We cannot create a culture of dialogue if we do not have identity'. Catholic institutions are increasingly involved in discussions about what constitutes Catholic identity. The emphasis in the document is for Catholic educational institutions to have clear policies built upon legalistic and bureaucratic procedures and tools, both secular and ecclesiastical, as a way of defending and protecting Catholic identity. The focus of these proposed recommended regulations concerns the employment of teachers who are to uphold Catholic teaching but may experience a growing range of internal rules and protocols which could result in legal challenges. Little is said about any philosophical basis for this identity which is to be secured through better regulation and more explicit policies. This might look like an attempt to substitute a philosophy of education by sheer authority.

Catholic Identity

The notion of Catholic identity has become a problem because its substantive content and the means to maintain it are not as clearly understood today. The 'Instruction' sums it up:

> The basic problem [of divergent interpretations of Catholic school identity] lies in the concrete application of the term 'Catholic', a complex word that is not easily expressed by means of exclusively legal, formal, and doctrinal criteria. The causes of tensions are mainly the result on the one hand of a *reductive* or purely *formal* interpretation and on the other of a vague or narrow understanding of Catholic identity.

The word Catholic is derived from the Greek phrase *kath'holou* meaning 'according to the whole' and it is intended to foster unity in the four central marks of the Church – one, holy, catholic, and apostolic. Catholic schools ought also to be marked by these four central Catholic pillars, but without eroding authentic differences, by means of a coherent diversity.

Dialogue

The other main theme of the document is 'dialogue'. Dialogue is central to the papacy of Pope Francis and can be understood as witnessing to one's faith but being open to the religious and non-religious beliefs of others. It is about sharing with others to better understand our similarities and differences and to dispel misconceptions and misunderstandings. Dialogue has its own challenges since it requires the navigation of various individual perspectives, value systems and a people's sense of identity. Such navigation can create discomfort, and, in some countries, dialogue is almost impossible. Dialogue with different philosophical positions is also sometimes impossible as not every philosophical stance is open to dialogue. The question arises of how you can strengthen identity while simultaneously remaining open to diversity and dialogue. How can you have maximal openness to the world and maximal hospitality towards others in all their diversity while articulating a preferential place for the Catholic tradition? You cannot affirm the value and equality of all religious identities without some stripping away of Catholic identity possibly resulting in minimal Catholic identity. If Catholic education can mean practically anything, then it becomes the serious study of nothing. We need to establish philosophical limits. As Redpath (2005) says:

> To develop a philosophy of education as Catholics, we must realize that Catholic faith must illumine such a philosophy. We must build it upon a Catholic understanding of the human person, the supernatural ends of the human person, and the means to achieve these ends.
> (see Hancock, 2017)

Perhaps the most important form of dialogue is between those who share the Catholic faith because what is urgently needed is a respectful conversation among the different factions within the Catholic education field.

Partial Philosophies

A variety of partial philosophies of Catholic education have arisen in practice over time and the question is what to make of this diversity. What criterion is needed to judge between them? This has not been assisted by the fact that the foundational culture of the West has been eroded, leading to confusion and anxiety (Rist and Rist, 2022). Education has fomented this confusion and what is striking about so much contemporary Catholic thought is how little 'thought' is in it. There appears to be a replacement of theology and philosophy by history, psychology, economics, and the social sciences as the Church's fundamental ways of thinking and seeing – often referred to as sociologism. A sociologism that may exclude not only God, but being, nature and truth. In a way this development mirrors the earlier-mentioned decline of traditional philosophy within contemporary 'philosophy of education' and its replacement with new assumptions rooted in social theory.

Since the Vatican has not called for a particular approach to philosophy of Catholic education, Catholic educators have consequently not sought to identify a distinct and single philosophy of Catholic education. Indeed, Dearden (1982), in an earlier survey of philosophies of education, had already concluded that there had been no explicit articulation of a philosophy of Catholic education since the 1950s. Today the Church calls for 'clearer awareness and consistency of the Catholic identity of the Church's educational institutions all over the world' (2022) but admits that despite numerous lay consultations, experts, and conferences, no such universal identity has been forthcoming. This raises difficulties since to simultaneously seek a distinctive identity without a corresponding philosophy of education is problematic. Nevertheless, there is a need for a broad definition of Catholic education that can encompass the Christian philosophical tradition and the Catholic theological tradition. There have been some, such as Donlon (1952: 18) in his *Theology of Education,* who believed that 'Catholic educators can claim no complete philosophy of education because no such thing exists. There is only a theology of Catholic education'. Etienne Gilson (1948) and Jacques Maritain (1943), both lay Catholic Frenchmen, argued for Christian philosophy's legitimacy and Gilson believed that there is a genuine 'Christian philosophy' which is not theology. Gilson (1948) presented the problem thus: '… it is simply a question of knowing whether to admit or deny that the exercise of natural reason, assisted by Revelation, is still a natural exercise of it, and whether the philosophy it begets still deserves the name philosophy'. Gilson answers with a decisive 'yes'. But others argued that the Christian philosopher ought not to combine anything deriving from Christianity into their philosophy, for then it passes over into theology.

McLaughlin (2002), who later occupied R. S. Peters's old Chair at the Institute of Education in London, rightly identifies the manifest difficulties and challenges of attempting to articulate a philosophy of Catholic education and situates such an attempt in the complex and multifaceted richness of the Catholic tradition of faith and life. He recognised that any philosophy of Catholic education must flow from a Catholic philosophy of life – the basic way Catholics look at reality. His recommendations are tentative and modest, arguing that the Catholic faith tradition provided ample sources for us to explore what an adequate contemporary Catholic conception of education might look like. G. K. Chesterton (1950) once wrote that

> Every education teaches a philosophy, if not by dogma, then by suggestion, by implication, by atmosphere. Every part of that education has a connection with every other part. If it does not all combine to convey some general view of life it is not education at all.

What is this 'general view of life' for Catholics? All education presupposes and involves a definite concept of human beings and life – it will have an underlying anthropology. In the Catholic sense of education, this anthropology begins with a theology of education which sets out some fundamental principles for a Catholic education.

Anthropology and Theology

Anthropology is, most simply, the study of human beings through time and space, particularly in relation to social practices including language, customs, and material culture. The new Dicastery for Culture and Education at the Vatican states that it 'works for the development of people's human values in the context of Christian anthropology'. In contrast, the more dominant academic view of anthropology found in universities is secular in orientation and has no space for a normative Christian anthropology. As Wulf (2002) observes 'The field of educational anthropology is therefore bound to be relative and fractional, provisional and limited' and it understands human activity on its own relativist terms excluding recourse to any theological beliefs. What is clear is that a distinctive Catholic anthropology is in its infancy and is slowly developing an education subfield. I can only here present a summary outline of this Christian anthropology within a problematic modern context in which the overlap between Catholicism and culture is disappearing. Multiple disciplines in the social sciences study and have a view of human nature but together offer no consistent idea of what it is to be human partly because they often know nothing of each other. In addition, the inner and most profound part of being human is often untouched by these studies whether they be biological, psychological, educational, social, economic, cultural, or any others. The pseudogods of instrumental culture can never meet the needs of a human being.

To gain a clear view of what the goals and purpose of Catholic education, it is helpful to answer questions about what human nature is. How we answer the question 'What does it mean to be human?' involves what we think about the nature of God and the nature of reality. What we think about God will determine what we can do in education as all education is concerned with the fulfilment of our human potentialities. Here we are concerned about what Christianity or Christian theology has to say about human beings. We can therefore begin with Catholic theological anthropology which teaches us that all human beings are created 'in the image' and 'after the likeness' of God (Gen 1: 26) composite of a united body and soul – male and female. Human beings are good and have intrinsic dignity and value as persons (Gen 1: 31). Human beings are free and are gifted with intellect and reason to discern and judge, but above all to come to know and contemplate God. This freedom grows over time and involves the capacity to know the truth, to choose good and to avoid evil. Christian faith believes that all humans are called by God 'to be conformed to the image of his Son' (Rom 8: 29–30), to 'put on Christ' and to 'be transformed into the likeness of Christ'. Christ 'is the way, the truth and the life' (Jn 14: 6). Catholic education, therefore, needs to be based on a distinctive Catholic anthropology derived from its own understanding of the nature and destiny of the human person. There are many anthropologies such as the sociological, the psychological, the economical, and so on by which people see and understand humanity. In contrast to these normally secularised anthropologies, a Christian anthropology goes beyond our materiality.

A Catholic anthropology teaches that human beings are called to God in the sense that human beings come from God through creation and return to God in our journey back to Him. No one is excluded from being human on the grounds of sex, nationality, or belief since we are all from a single family and despite our diversity and different conditions, we share a common humanity. We learn more about ourselves through our relationship with others. God created us with the potential for human wisdom and – in other words we are endowed with the capacity to reason and therefore are capable of being educated in both a broad and narrow sense. Indeed, human rationality distinguishes the human species from other living species. Christ affirms the validity of humanity, for Christ became perfectly human. Catholic anthropology is not simply seen in the light of human reason but also in Christian revelation which provides us with a lens to identify what is going wrong in alternative anthropologies.

Hancock (2017) describes this when he says that Catholic education rests on a truth about the human person: a truth radiating out of the Gospel with five sign points: (1) a union of body and soul; (2) a creature possessing an intellect and will, whereby it is stamped with the image of God; (3) a being of conscience called to a moral destiny; (4) a creature who is soul by nature, whose own identity is tied in some way to the identities and lives of others; and finally (5) someone God desires to save, a creature whose happiness ultimately depends on ordering its life around things of God. The central goal of Catholic educators is therefore the *integral formation of the human person*. This results in a synthesis of faith and life with the ends of Catholic education focused on the spiritual, the moral, and the religious. This entails the promotion of a philosophical-theological position that has been codified in the Catechism of the Catholic Church and in her Creeds. Therefore, a philosophy of Catholic education must have its roots first in an anthropology and a theology of education.

This Catholic theology entails a belief in a living God, specifically in Jesus Christ in whose life God was made known and was present. Theology explains what human beings are made to be. The Church claims to be in possession of a body of knowledge or revealed truths which explain our place in creation and our relationship with the Creator. This relationship is in and through Jesus Christ, whose life and work can alone lead us to God. The life of faith on earth is therefore a preparation for our eternal destiny with God. The Catholic believes that God is holy and we, being created in the image of God, must attempt by grace to reflect that holiness in our lives. This belief in God affects the choices we make, the relationships we forge, the lifestyles we adopt and the attitudes and behaviours we exhibit. The question for the Christian is not 'How ought we to live?' but rather 'How ought we, who have been gifted by God, to live?' To love God and one's neighbour as oneself is the general moral aim for a Christian (Arthur, 2021). Each human being is born with an essential core of goodness, dignity, and value and is called to seek the flourishing of self and others through love and service. Each person is intrinsically relational and formed through life by relationships. The catechism emphasises the inherent social nature of human beings and this goes beyond the context in which the individual acts, as it states: 'Society is not for him an extraneous addition but a requirement of his nature' (#1879). Modern educational philosophies, even those that see themselves as grounded in social theorising, often assume an atomistic, autonomous individual as the ideal resulting in the idea of man as an *alter Deus*, that is a quasi-creator of his or her world – something contrary to Catholic teaching.

Each human being is a body-soul unified with a unique personal identity that develops over time in a particular cultural context. Importantly, everyone suffers from the effects of original sin, but is invited to divine redemption in Jesus Christ. Our ability to know and love God can be distorted through sin but can also be restored through grace. Each human being bears the dignity of being made in the image of God and this dignity is promoted when, aided by God's grace, we choose to perform good human acts. Good is done when a person acts in a way that is authentically human, and a good life makes flourishing possible. In short, we are created, fallen, and redeemed. There is the Christian faith conviction that we as humans have a common telos; there is an ultimate common good, or highest good, that is God, and the life in God through the Resurrection of Jesus Christ. This teleological movement shapes human life from conception to life and its endpoint is relationship with God. To make his redemptive work available to successive generations, along with channels of grace, Christ established an authoritative means of transmission and mediation. That is the Church itself.

Scripture is a clear source for a philosophy of Catholic education. The modern trend has been to refer to Gospel Values in justifying a Catholic education's mission, but this is an expansive phrase that attempts to encompass everything. There is no official list to choose from or that must be embraced. There appears to be complete freedom to choose what Gospel Values correspond to what any institution aims to do and the connection to Scripture is not always made clear. The commendable zeal of such appeals to Gospel Values is not always matched by clarity regarding how we are to relate the Scriptures to educational practices. The values that Catholic educational institutions choose include service, truth, justice, compassion, hope, love, peace, involvement, empathy, courage, acceptance, tolerance, belonging, caring, temperance, sacrifice, stewardship, concern, patience, optimism, human dignity, respect, self-esteem, commitment, and so on. There is no priority or ranking given to these values other than the set that is chosen. Contrary to both Aristotle and

Aquinas, no master or meta-virtues are identified for the purposes of adjudication when these individual virtues collide. Nor is there usually an explanation of why these values have been selected rather simply a statement or assertion of the values themselves. MacIntyre (1971: 24) argued that

> Injunctions to repent, to be responsible, even to be generous, do not actually tell us what to do ... Christians behave like everyone else but use a different vocabulary in characterizing their behavior, and so conceal their lack of distinctiveness ... All those in our society who self-consciously embrace beliefs which appear to confer importance and righteousness upon the holder become involved in the same strategies. The fact that their beliefs make so little difference either to them or to others leads to the same concern with being right-minded rather than effective.

Paul warns us in scripture about the use of philosophy: 'Make sure that no one traps you and deprives you of your freedom by some second-hand, empty, rational philosophy based on principles of this world instead of on Christ' (Col, 2:8). By this he meant that we should not be taken capture by a particular kind of philosophy. Peter says: 'always have your answer ready for people who ask you the reason for the hope that you all have' (I Pet, 3:15). It is necessary for us to provide responses to alternative philosophical positions. It is why C. S. Lewis observed in a sermon he gave at the Church of St Mary the Virgin in Oxford in 1941, that 'Good philosophy must exist, if for no other reason, because bad philosophy must be answered'.

The Catholic tradition has long appropriated the importance of philosophy for its defence and support. Catholics have known since the early patristic period that rational and philosophical support for the faith is both necessary and possible. Titus Flavius Clemens (150–215), otherwise known as Clement of Alexandria, was an early Church writer who converted to the Catholic faith and was the first to use Greek philosophy combined with Scripture. Philosophy began in the classical world to rationally explain key questions, such as: what is man? What constitutes a good life? What are the ends of human life? Clement had been fully educated within a pagan culture at a time when the Church did not establish schools, content to use the classical education delivered by pagan schools. He believed that the classical education available in the pagan world excelled at perfecting man's natural abilities, something that could not be said with confidence about education today.

The Church saw the Catechumenate, formation, and preparation for baptism, as fulfilling the role of Catholic education. However, Clement played an important part in the evolution of a philosophy of Catholic education since his aim was to make Christianity intelligible to those in the Greek tradition. He wanted educated Christians who could debate with pagans – a sort of dialogue with the contemporary culture you could say. We find ourselves today in an increasingly non-Christian culture much like the Church in the second century.

Clement saw philosophy as a gift from God and wanted to use it to benefit the Church; therefore, he taught that we should not fear philosophy. Clement also held education in high regard and established his Catechetical School in Alexandria which taught secular subjects. His book *Paedagogus* was the first systematic writing of Christian education. Faith and knowledge, he believed, should work together but that education should ultimately lead the learner to intimacy with God. Origen of Alexandria, another Christian philosopher–theologian, subsequently promoted an integration of Platonic philosophy and Christianity just as Justin Martyr had done before Clement. All three believed that all truth is God's truth wherever it is found, and they worked to overcome some of the suspicions Christians had of pagan education.

There were of course Christians who disagreed with this approach, such as Tertullian, who asked rhetorically 'What indeed has Athens got to do with Jerusalem?' He answered 'nothing' because he believed that once you find Christ, you have no need for philosophy. This was a claim that purely philosophy-based answers are redundant for Christianity. However, many early Church Fathers believed the opposite – that Greek philosophy prepared people for understanding the faith, to better understand the faith and to defend the faith. It is interesting that Maritain (1962: 19) believed that God prepared the way for the Gospels by making the Greeks the chosen people of reason, and the Jews the chosen people of faith. Not something that the early Church Fathers would have written, but they would have understood philosophy as a bridge – common ground for discussion between believers and non-believers as well as helping non-believers to cross over to the faith. Many Church Fathers did however call the writings of Plato and Aristotle the precursors to the Gospel. It is also important to bear in mind here that much of what a thinker such as Dewey defines as 'educational philosophy' addresses practical (but still philosophically illuminating) questions of classroom implementation and teaching methods – where one might not expect Catholic philosophy of education to offer any uniquely Christian perspective.

Augustine (354–430), another convert and Roman citizen born Aurelius Augustinus Hipponensis, recognised that in any conflict between faith and reason, faith must predominate. Nevertheless, in his writings, he accommodated several philosophical perspectives. Augustine understood that this world is not where we finally belong, but we are part of it. We therefore choose and decide our destiny within it. He taught that we should seek an educational philosophy that is coherent with the true nature of the human person and for Augustine that was to make true Disciples of Christ. Augustine described the role of the catechist and explained how catechumens should be educated. He explained a philosophy of how we 'learn' in *De Magistro* and in his *Confessions* described his own self-education in the faith. Augustine used the Greek and Roman classical tradition in a limited way and placed it firmly within a theological framework. We should remember that Augustine had resigned his post as the prestigious imperial professor of rhetoric at Milan because he was disillusioned, he complained that classical education in the later Roman Empire had become fragmented and professionalised, indeed, it had become purposeless, focused on fame and career – much like the academy today.

While Augustine was critical of certain aspects of pagan education, he used the metaphor of the 'gold of the Egyptians' to say that just as the Jews were allowed by God to plunder the gold of their Egyptian captors when they left slavery, so, too, are Christians allowed to make use of the wisdom of pagan writers so long as it does not contradict Christian truth. Philosophical insights from the Greeks and Romans could be used to explain, elaborate, and communicate the faith, but faith always outweighed anything in classical philosophy for Augustine. Augustine's approach was always more theological than philosophical. Therefore, education and learning have the twin aims of serving our temporal welfare and promoting our eternal good.

The Church Fathers claimed some connection between sacred and secular learning. Today, many Catholic philosophers of education have little hesitancy in accommodating and embracing many secular philosophical positions in what they would describe as their 'Catholic philosophy'. They have an open-ended approach in the search for truth and a tolerance of all values and assumptions regarding the truths so discovered. They tend to make generic statements and keep the faith dimensions of their philosophies implicit and largely unexpressed. We live in a purposeless world of materialism in which many philosophical presuppositions are generally antagonistic to Catholicism. A world in which individuals increasingly are defined by what they feel themselves to be inside and act in accordance with these feelings.

McLaughlin et al. (1996: 139) wrote that what is needed is a 'distinctively Catholic philosophy of education to be developed which can draw upon the philosophical resources of notable Catholic thinkers such as Aquinas, Newman, Maritain, Chesterton, Lonergan, but which will address directly matters of current educational concern'. Of course, there are many more: Clement of Alexandria, Augustine, St. Benedict, Abelard, St. Bernard of Clairvaux, William of Ockham, Dun Scotus, St Ignatius of Loyola, Erasmus, Pascal, Descartes, De Maistre, Blondel, Anscombe, MacIntyre, Kreeft to name but a few. It is impossible to cover all these thinkers and what they have to offer us in constructing a philosophy of Catholic education. Whittle (2014) also reviews the work of some modern theologians, such as Rahner and Lonergan, on the relationship between Catholic education and theology recognising that the link has been traditionally understated. A detailed and integrated Catholic idea of the person can be found in the work of Vitz et al. (2020: 21–44). Should Catholic philosophers bring their faith commitments with them so that it is about their faith-seeking understanding?

The Church rejects any philosophy that teaches that what people know should be divorced from who they are and how they live. A key feature of Catholic education is the central importance of cultivating a life of prayer, transcendence, and a deepening of one's communion and friendship with God.

Formation in the spiritual life is an essential characteristic of Catholic education. The purpose of Catholic education therefore should be the fullness of human flourishing which must include holiness. Education is also about learning how to become wise. There is also a Catholic emphasis on the community as a means of education. Full human flourishing is marked not only by growth in intellectual and cognitive skills but also by growth in wisdom – in the ability to discern what is truly important to live a good human life. Perfect flourishing is reserved for heaven, but we have the capacity on earth to flourish in some way in relationship with God and neighbour. Catholic educators are called to assist in the formation and development of their students' moral conscience.

> True education is directed towards the formation of the human person in view of his final end and the good of that society to which he belongs and in the duties of which he will, as an adult, have a share.
> (Second Vatican Council, 1965: 1)

And

> [T]he Church ... reaffirm[s] her mission of education to insure strong character formation... It ... stimulates her to foster truly Christian living and apostolic communities, equipped to make their own positive contribution, in a spirit of cooperation, to the building up of the secular society.
> (CCE, 1977: 11)

The formational process often involves the head – knowledge of the faith, the heart – experience of living the faith, and the hands – the practice of enacting the faith. The aim is not simply to be smarter, but wiser and genuinely a good person.

Mary Boys (1989: 132) casts serious doubt on whether an all-embracing philosophy of Catholic education is possible, but in the absence of a single philosophy she identifies some inter-related dimensions of Catholic education:

> The educational philosophy of post-Vatican II Roman Catholicism derives, first, from the characteristics of Catholicism itself; second, from the statements and publications of various official and quasi-official bodies (e.g., national episcopal conferences, ...); and, third, from the corporate life of various forms of Catholic communal life (e.g., schools as "faith communities," diocesan agencies, justice centres, and other alternative educational institutions), especially as these communities struggle to formulate and embody ideals in "mission statements." Together they form a certain consistent pattern that deserves more detailed analysis.

She (1989: 141) also observes:

> To the outsider, post-conciliar Catholic educational philosophy may seem amazingly consistent in its emphasis on faith communities orientated towards the creation of more just societies. But the Catholic penchant for documentation may be misleading, insofar as it suggests more coherence than exists in reality.

The diversity of Catholic philosophies of education indicates that there is no one single formulation of Catholic education. However, once a particular Catholic institution settles on its own philosophy of education it takes a theological stand. The institution has an identifiable theology of education, which may or may not correspond to the teachings of the Catholic Church or even to the theological propositions which are the self-declared basis of its own mission and identity. In simple language, what Boys is saying is that she rejects the philosophical understanding of Catholicism as standing over and against the world and advocates that ultimately Catholic educators must trust in their own direction. In this she has captured the trajectory of Catholic education in modern times.

Catholic philosophy in its essence is concerned with the mystery of being and its import for the question of our relationship to ourselves, the world, and the Divine. Therefore, we need to explain the essentials of education in the light of the Christian philosophy of life. The roots of a philosophy of Catholic education are grounded in Catholic theology and the rich heritage of Jewish and Greek roots, early Church Father's, Scholastic philosophers and theologians, Renaissance humanists, and the work of countless Catholic philosophers and theologians. Catholic education integrates the truths of human learning discoverable by human reason, with the truths of revelation known only by faith, so that the believer may serve God and man in this world in preparation for the next. Belief in the world to come is the key belief that undergirds this theology of education. John Paul II (1998) says in *Fides et Ratio* that 'the Church has no philosophy of her own nor does she canonize any one philosophy in preference to others'. Does this mean the Church supports unlimited philosophical pluralism? Is there a free for all in philosophy? No, because the basic Catholic anthropology includes the following essentials that have all been alluded to above (see Arthur, 2021): (1) a union of body and soul, (2) a creature possessing intellect and will, (3) a being of conscience called to a moral destiny, (4) a creature whose own identity is tied in some way to the identities and lives of others, and (5) someone God desires to save.

What Is 'Catholic' about Catholic Education

As has already become clear, the Church may accommodate a multiplicity of different philosophies of education if they are receptive to the doctrinal teachings of the Church. A diversity of philosophical perspectives on Catholic education needs to be commensurable with the Catholic faith. How are different conceptions of Catholic education adequate as possible expressions of the Christian faith? In what ways can there be similarity in diversity or unity in multiplicity?

Thomas Groome (2021) in *What Makes Catholic Education Catholic*, says that 'Catholic schools educate from a faith perspective and for a faith perspective'. He makes clear that this has nothing to do with imposing ideas on students, but rather is about inviting students 'to consider a spiritual grounding for their lives in the world that might make their lives a little more meaningful, worthwhile, purposeful, ethical, and might sustain them in tough times'. No mention of evangelisation or catechesis here. However, there are important issues, not least about how Catholic institutions can transmit their values in a context of religious pluralism and where non-Catholics, sometimes the majority, make up the population of Catholic institutions. How do we approach the question of evangelisation in religiously diverse contexts? Pope Francis has confirmed that Catholic education is evangelisation. He told the Christian Brothers in May 2022 to evangelise by educating and educate by evangelisation. He concluded his remarks with:

> It is your way of realizing what Saint Paul wrote: "Christ is formed in you" (Gal 4:19). To educate in this way is your apostolate, your specific contribution to evangelization: to make the person grow according to Christ. In this sense, your schools are "Christian": not because of an external label, but because they take this path …. Thank you for what you are and what you do! Go forth with the joy of evangelizing by educating and of educating by evangelizing. I bless you and all your communities.

It might be noted in passing that the word evangelisation evokes some negative reaction among those who prefer to focus on the ecumenical dimensions of the documents in Vatican II.

The Declaration on Christian Education at Vatican II, *Gravissimum Educationis*, is clear that the primary function of a Catholic school is to evangelise and that education is a means to that end. The 1997 guidance to Catholic schools, *Catholic Schools on the Threshold of the Third Millennium*, while laying out numerous issues and problems, still insists that Catholic educational institutions ought to have a 'missionary thrust' with a 'fundamental duty to evangelise' and 'to go towards men and women wherever they are, so that they may receive the gift of salvation'. According to the Church' Canon Law, a 'Catholic school is understood as one which a competent ecclesiastical authority or a public ecclesiastical juridic person directs or which ecclesiastical authority recognizes as such through a written document' (Can. 803, § 1) and that 'instruction and education in a Catholic school must be grounded in the principles of Catholic doctrine; teachers are to be outstanding in correct doctrine and integrity of life' (Can. 803, § 2). This canon concludes that 'even if it is in fact Catholic, no school is to bear the name Catholic school without the consent of competent ecclesiastical authority' (Can. 803, § 3). Catholic schools do not therefore exist for mere excellence in reading and writing – they cannot be simply rooted in secular success. They exist to teach the student to be a good Catholic and to live out their faith in the world. Teachers in Catholic schools are seen as more than employees – they are seen as part of the Church's mission and are therefore ministers in the name of the Church. The recent 2022 document from the Vatican concerned as it is with pastoral and theological questions warns against Catholic schools avoiding the use of the word Catholic in their mission statements. However, even for those who endorse this essential guidance, various questions remain that fall under the standard remit for 'educational philosophy' and about which Catholic educational thinkers cannot feign ignorance.

Catholic educational institutions are generally linked to a Catholic religious ethos and sacramental tradition. In this perspective, the school is an ecclesial community and should have a sacramental culture that helps shape what students see as reality. Schools often prepare students for the sacraments of confession, Holy Communion, and confirmation – a process called sacramental catechesis. A key feature of education in a Catholic school is the central importance of cultivating a life of prayer, transcendence, and a deepening of one's communion and friendship with God. Formation in the spiritual life is an essential characteristic of Catholic education. The purpose of Catholic education therefore should be the fullness of human flourishing which must include holiness. Indeed, holiness is a central goal of Catholic education. The central aspiration of education in a Catholic school is to become saints, that is, to live the life of Christ as revealed in the Gospels and lived out as Church. Catholic schools follow the customs and practices of the Church to nourish the spirituality and faith of students and staff.

Education is also learning how to become wise. There is a Catholic emphasis on the community as a means of education. Full human flourishing is marked not only by growth in intellectual and cognitive skills but also by growth in wisdom – in the ability to discern what is truly important to live a good human life. Catholic schools are called to assist in the formation and development of their students' moral conscience.

> True education is directed towards the formation of the human person in view of his final end and the good of that society to which he belongs and in the duties of which he will, as an adult, have a share.
> (Second Vatican Council, 1965: 1)

And

> [T]he Church ... reaffirm[s] her mission of education to insure strong character formation... It ... stimulates her to foster truly Christian living and

apostolic communities, equipped to make their own positive contribution, in a spirit of cooperation, to the building up of the secular society.

(CCE, 1977: 11)

Being Christian embraces 'being for others' and 'being with others' in community.

Conclusion

If education is a lifelong process of learning how to return to God, our creator, and a route to being transformed into the likeness of Christ, then we need theology to help us search for the meaning of education. A philosophy of Catholic education can be open to the non-Christian and can expand the vision of what it means to be a human being. In summary, when exploring the nature of the human person, the Christian tradition has emphasised both the material as well as the spiritual aspects of humankind. To lessen one at the expense of the other leaves us with a partial, and in some cases distorted picture of human nature. Kelty (1999: 22) has argued that there has been a shift from philosophy to theology in understanding Catholic education. He quotes Groppo (1991: 440) in outlining four challenges for a contemporary theology of education:

> First is the evaluation of the educational problems which culture presents to faith; second is the critical appropriation of modern theology's understanding of salvation, holiness, autonomy, human action, and education as liberating and humanizing processes; third is the understanding of the process of religious conversion and development; fourth is the description of the parameters of maturity and growth in both developmental and religious terms.

Forming lives of faith, hope, and love in the light of Jesus Christ is, therefore, part of the evangelising mission of the Catholic Church and must be understood in terms of, and in line with that mission (see Haldane, 2023). The main goal of education is therefore to help human beings fully realise their nature as rational and spiritual beings, premised on a theistic philosophy of education underpinned by the following principles (see Arthur, 2021):

1. God created everything that exists, including human beings, which confers an objective order on reality in which we have the capacity to know and understand.
2. All human beings share a common nature which participates in spiritual and material realities, but their education is differentiated, changing over time through various stages of life.
3. Every person's life is an expression of purposeful movement towards a goal.

4   These norms are grounded in human nature, and human beings cannot flourish or be genuinely fulfilled if they ignore them.
5   Education is the complete formation of a person through the realisation of certain potentialities that lead to a mature human being.
6   Human flourishing is always the end of individual human action, and the good life depends on reasonable action exercised by everyone.
7   The human being is a free moral agent and responsible for their own actions.
8   There is an indelible core of goodness and dignity in each human person.
9   While the good life is the purpose of human life in this world the human being is a being for God, and God is found in the world.
10 Education aids human beings to experience being in the presence of God.
11 Human beings act more humanely when reasoning, but this is always incomplete and imperfect.
12 Christian conscience is formed by fundamental theological virtues, particularly faith, hope and love.
13 The good life consists of intrinsically excellent virtues which give rise to activities that education cultivates.
14 The intellectual virtues should aid the study of logic, critical thinking and the scientific method, and education should teach students to understand reality. Humans have a natural desire and need for knowledge.

Catholic education prepares human beings for life, and as stated above, the main goal of education is to help us become full human persons. The educational process behind this formation becomes a practical expression of one's theological commitments as a Christian and will influence how we believe, think, learn, act, and treat each other. Education aims to foster the highest degree of excellence attainable by those who receive it, however variable that attainment may be given the particularities of each individual. Catholic education may draw on some of the best elements of some secular approaches to educational philosophy but needs always to venture beyond them. The human nature assumed by God the Son shows that Catholics embrace all natural goods, such that Catholic education should rightly explore the sciences, human wisdom, everything knowable by the human mind working on its own. But the supernatural elevation of Christ's human nature also shows our supernatural end and the *grace* needed to overcome the effects of sin that obscure our intellects and disfigure our character: only with God's help can human nature reach its proper perfection and reach beyond its own powers to achieve its supernatural end.

2 Charisms, Definitions, and Models of Catholic Education

The opening chapter discussed what philosophy of education has been in the Church, academy in the past and its decline, and after that what the Church is currently left with in terms of a rationale or basis for Catholic education. We will proceed to what can be brought from philosophy to improve that, starting with Thomism (Chapter 3) and then going on to a critical appropriation from other philosophies (Chapter 4). This chapter will consider certain Catholic themes, such as religious charisms, and definitions of constants, such as evangelisation and mission, liberal formation and integral education, catechesis, and identity, in Catholic education as well as various contemporary models of Catholic education. Each one of these themes and approaches is essential source to understand the distinctiveness of Catholic education. This chapter continues the exploration of Catholic rationales found in Chapter 1 of what further tools the Church can use to advance an authentic development of Catholic education. It begins with a discussion of religious charisms in education.

Religious Charisms and Education

Religious charisms are special gifts of the Holy Spirit and may characterise an individual or group. A charism is the core value that normally emanates from a Religious Order and is distinctive of that Order. It refers to the special spirit that animates a religious community and gives it a particular character. You could say that a charism is the permanent heritage of a community which includes its rule, mission, history, and traditions. However, it can be elusive and lacking in clarity to those who are not members or educated in the religious community. The term was first used by Pope Paul VI in reference to Religious Orders but was later extended to their work in educational institutions. The charism would often link to the founder but could also develop in response to changing conditions in society and culture. Some also refer to the charisms of schools run by the laity in the belief that they also can conceptualise their core values in terms of charisms to strengthen their distinctiveness. This raises the question of what the charisms of lay Catholics are and how these are formed.

DOI: 10.4324/9781003486435-3

This chapter has been made available under a CC-BY-NC-ND 4.0 license.

Six religious orders or communities have been selected below to give a flavour of the variety of different charisms that are advocated today – some believe that since charisms are a living reality, they continue to change in response to a rapidly changing world, and this is reflected in their educational charisms. The six examples below show both change and continuity but are essentially modern interpretations of religious charism employing some contemporary language from the general culture. Each list is drawn randomly from various websites:

Benedictine:

Love of Christ and neighbour
Prayer
Stability
Conversion – meaning transformation
Obedience – meaning listening and changing
Discipline
Humility
Hospitality
Stewardship
Community – meaning the common good

Franciscan:

Education is incarnational
Education is personal
Education is transformative
Education engages the heart
Education develops servant leaders
Education pursues wisdom
Peace-making, service, poverty, simplicity, and reverence for all creation

Dominican:

Study
Prayer
Community
Evangelisation

Jesuit:

Education:
Is world affirming
Assists in the total formation of everyone within the human community

Includes a religious dimension
Is an apostolic instrument
Promotes dialogue between faith and culture

For Jesuits the learning outcome is identified in five C's. Our education must make our students persons of Conscience, Competence, Compassion, Commitment, and Character.

Salesian:

Educator perceived as father, mother, brother, sister, guide, and protector
Three principles – reason, religion, and loving-kindness

Lasallian:

Faith in the presence of God.
Concern for the poor and social justice
Respect for all persons
Quality education
Inclusive community

How are these charisms related to the essential characteristics of Catholic education? Do they represent a philosophy of Catholic education in themselves? Is there, for instance, a separate Jesuit Catholic philosophy of education? How far have they been influenced by secular philosophies of education? Many of these charisms can be interpreted as schools purposefully offering a caring community within a social context that promotes feelings of belonging and being affirmed as people as well as working for justice and peace through social activism and caring for creation. The problem is that none of this is unique to a Catholic school and says little about a Church-cantered theology of mission. An alternative would be for the school to see itself as part of the Church's mission that includes these largely social charisms but ensures that Catholic beliefs are taught as part of a catechetical and sacramental education and formation. The Benedictine charism, for example, saw reading and writing within a larger orbit of the Christian life. It is grounded in Catholic anthropology, has a Catholic worldview, and is shaped by a spirituality of communion. This charism approach to aiding the construction of a Catholic philosophy of education has potential, but they are all dependent on competing theological visions. How do we then determine the main characteristics of Catholic education?

Definitions

There are several interrelated and complementary definitions, themes, or dimensions in Catholic education that are repeatedly highlighted in any survey of official Church documents. The following are consistently identified: (1) mission and evangelisation, (2) catechesis and identity, and (3) liberal formation and integral education. Each of these themes make an essential contribution to working out a philosophy of Catholic education. They are therefore worth unpacking by way of definition and interpretation as unique characteristics of Catholic education. However, it should be recognised that there is considerable slippage in what they mean as the same words are used with different meanings rooted in diverse philosophies of life. There are also other terms such as 'dialogue', 'charism', 'love', 'mercy', 'service', and 'accompaniment' as well as 'education for the poor' and 'diversity' that are also seen as part of the characteristics or goals of Catholic education and are increasingly mentioned in official Church documents. Catholic schools and universities will highlight a selection of these terms in their mission statements which combined with some theological terms, it is claimed, give them a unique exceptionalism among contemporary educational institutions.

Mission and Evangelisation

Mission always signals an aim or undertaking, and this aim for the Church is summarised in Matthew 28: 19–20: 'go therefore and make disciples of all nations'. Christ is the reason for the existence of Catholic educational institutions, and they are integral agents in the mission of the Church. They need to be authentic places of encounter with Christ and have a clear purpose as ecclesial entities to bring faith, culture, and life into harmony with each other. They are places that illuminate reason, enliven culture, and give meaning to learning. They collectively strive to meet the challenge of Matthew's Gospel.

It is the responsibility of all believers to spread the Gospel, and this process is called evangelisation. Pope Francis in a June 2018 address said, 'Schools and Universities need to be consistent and show continuity between their foundational mission and the Church's mission of evangelisation'. Evangelisation is indeed a fundamental mission of the Church, and therefore, evangelisation is not solely within the purview of a Catholic institution since the role of the broader ecclesial community must not be overlooked. We must acknowledge that there is a deep divide between Church and modern culture and that Catholic institutions have both an academic and religious purpose, and it is the latter that sets it apart from other institutions. Moreover, Christ is the standard and measure of a school or university's Catholicity.

Catechesis and Identity

Catechesis is a formative process of transmitting the Gospel, and the optimal setting for such catechesis is not an academic community but rather a community of believers. Nevertheless, Catholic schools have been locations for children to be prepared for first communion and confirmation. They also provide religious education which is often seen as being identical to catechesis with the explicit aim of educating in the faith. The role of the Catholic school is to nurture those who are baptised and are already actively engaged with the Catholic tradition together with those who are not yet engaged in a journey of faith. It not only concerns knowledge of the faith but also sharing and living the faith. In a Catholic institution, all may be immersed in the shared beliefs, language, symbols, liturgy, and worship of the Catholic tradition which help deepen the initial conversion to faith and is a lifelong process. Each student will gradually see things through the eyes of faith and move, perhaps, towards commitment to the faith. Knowing Christ is different from simply knowing about him. Catechesis is a form of ministry of the word and seeks to initiate the students into the teachings of Christian doctrine and the fullness of Christian life. It is not separate from the pastoral and catechetical work of the rest of the Church which also aims to increase faith. It needs to be recognised that education is not the same as catechesis, but while distinct, they are complementary to each other. The Vatican's 2022 'Instruction' makes clear that Catholic education is not strictly catechetical, nor is it a 'mere philanthropic work aimed at responding to a social need' but is an essential part of the Church's identity and mission.

It is a common belief today that you can possess a Catholic identity, for example as a 'cultural Christian', even if you do not share the understanding and beliefs with the Church's teachings. There are those in academia who, in varying degrees of explicitness, view all hierarchy and authority as oppressive and believe that all of humanity is connected and must have equal respect and concern as well as affirming the positive value of culture, pluralism, freedom, and democratic institutions. I, in no way, wish to pit myself against pluralism freedom or democracy or hide behind barred gates, but the more progressive Catholic outlook seeks ultimately to emancipate themselves from the supernatural and moral order of Catholicism, which includes moral and religious demands. They therefore see education as a distinct human activity that ought to have its own autonomy along the lines that Pring and Hirst outlined in the 1960s. The human being is simply a sophisticated animal with a large brain, and there is nothing beyond the material.

This line of thought simply encourages the segmentation of life that is associated with a process of secularisation. It conceives of Catholicism as an 'ism' among others and always seeks to value that which is on the other side of the boundaries, boundaries they often do not recognise. They believe there cannot be any criteria or common measurements to evaluate Catholic educational institutions and that they are merely institutions that are intended to provide an educational service to all, not only for Catholics, and therefore must not put in place any barriers to the inclusion of all. They generally have an egalitarian partial anthropology emphasising social justice that commonly procure facets from numerous philosophies of education. I believe some of these ideas as applied to Catholic educational institutions are utopian and non-sustainable over time and will lead to the demise of anything distinctly Catholic. At the same time, I believe in openness, particularly open inquiry, self-criticism, and internal dialogue. Nevertheless, a sense of Catholic identity can only be achieved through continuity commitments that provide a degree of certainty and direction in life.

Casson (2014) writes that there are many different Catholic identities that are developed by students in Catholic educational institutions and that these reflect a 'fragmentary view of Catholicity'. She lists eight identities that she found in Catholic schools: (1) Hardcore Catholic, (2) Baptised Catholic, (3) Halfway Catholic, (4) Catholic Pilgrim, (5) Golden Rule Catholic, (6) School Catholic, (7) Catholic Atheist, and (8) Family Catholic. She claims, wrongly, that the Catholic school is the only location where you can build such identities. In the past, Catholic institutions saw their religious identity through traditional forms of piety and sacramental practice, but this cannot be presumed today in either students or staff. Indeed, the Catholic school may be the only place where they have any familiarity with Catholic beliefs and values. In the Vatican's 'Instruction' (2022), it states clearly that there is a 'need for a clearer awareness and consistency of the Catholic identity of the Church's educational institutions throughout the world' and views the Church as 'mother and teacher'. The document, like previous Vatican documents, is concerned with regulating and bounding the experience of Catholic identity in Catholic institutions. The challenge is enormous especially as many students today, whether baptised or not, are loosely connected and weakly committed to the faith. Casson's work simply reinforces that there is a complex fluidity that defies categorisation because these teenagers have simply incorporated some traditional beliefs and practices with seemingly incompatible practices and beliefs. Even those who may be described as cultural Catholics are usually disconnected from a personal practice or commitment to Catholicism.

Van Beeck (1985) provides another set of models of Catholic identity, albeit rather distorted. The first is the pistic model, with identity defined by catechisms, rules, regulations, precepts, clergy dominance, authoritarianism, rigidity, and a past seen as the 'golden age'. The second model is the charismatic that understands Catholic identity in many forms with the institutional Church less important since personal experience is more important than authority. It is a model whose members do not welcome Church rules or guidance. The third model is the mystic that sees the mystical experience of faith as a gift from God, not the Church. Any model of identity seeks to convey or build an explanation of the underlying identity expressed by aiding definition and communicating a set of concepts that support further analysis. However, the model may not reflect the reality itself and may be part of a wider argument. For example, Beeck deliberately sets up his pistic model as a negative calling it a 'ghetto mentality' that needs to be avoided. It is not necessarily the case that teaching the catechism leads to an authoritarian approach.

Most secular or public schools form and develop their institutional identity spontaneously as they do not begin by defining their identity at the outset. The Catholic school by contrast ought to begin with prior commitments to certain truths of the faith, and therefore, institutional identity can be developed from a clear understanding of mission. From this, mission and vision of education policies and guidelines are developed to express the identity of the institution – this identity is articulated, expressed, and embedded in the institution through the minds and hearts of students and staff.

Liberal Formation and Integral Education

Formation is a process by which something comes into existence or begins to have a particular shape. Catholic human formation is about what it means to be human – all human beings are 'unique and unrepeatable'. It involves intellectual formation so that students understand the beliefs held by the Church and therefore requires the teaching of theology, philosophy, and history – a liberal education. Spiritual formation is the foundational practice of the faith, and this is shaped in a Christian community. It not only includes what is nowadays called character education but also goes beyond it. The school is a place where the human person ought to be affirmed and where education ought to be based on love with Christ as the foundation. However, there are those who see faith formation as an inclusive term meaning any faith and the role of Catholic schools is to encourage and facilitate students in practising and developing their understanding of their own religious beliefs from wherever background they come from. There are many who believe that formation ought to increase 'human capital' and the purpose is to transform society from the perspective of peace, justice, and love to serve the poor and victims of injustice (see Boatens, 2019). Catholic educational institutions are seen as having a twofold purpose of being necessary for the good of the Church and for the wider society (see Curren, 1997). They have not only a theological vision but also a social vision, but this approach often lacks symmetry.

Formation in virtue is another feature of Catholic education. This notion of Christian character transcends the temporal, the material, and the secular and points towards the eternal, the spiritual, and the religious. It is not simply about what ought I to do but also what ought I to *be* and *become*. Christians are called by God 'to be conformed to the image of his Son' (*Romans* 8:29–30). Christian character is the possession of those qualities that are essentially Godly – and thereby 'goodly'. Goodness does not exist apart from concrete expression. Human beings have a natural inclination to follow and pursue the good; in other words, we have a natural capacity to discern between good and evil. Good is done when a person acts in a way that is authentically human, and a good life makes flourishing possible. It follows, therefore, that the mind that is illuminated by God's grace and guided by reason will grow in good character. This transformative process is ongoing and lifelong and requires an openness, willingness, and commitment to be so transformed and a recognition of the fact that the route to goodness can be obscured and obstructed by our own failings.

The moral virtues of Christian character have an objective reality that does not depend on any person or group of people's opinions or beliefs about them. They are not good because we approve of them; rather we should approve of them because they are good in and of themselves. God's dealings with humanity provides the framework for understanding the conditions of human life. What God wills for a human being can be known, at least in part, by the observation of these conditions. Christian virtue formation is to live the faith by growing in virtue, dispositions animated by love. Virtues are the reason that a person performs good actions more easily, and they are a sign and cause of the goodness of a person. The goal of education is a lifelong process of learning how to (re)turn to God. Therefore, the primary aim of Christian formation is to assist students to become more faithful followers of Christ. Character virtues are needed to help us act in certain ways as disciples of Christ. The virtues enable us to act well and help us know and desire the good. Christian morality consists of living life with guidance and inspiration from the Christian scriptures, tradition, human reason, and experience. Christianity offers its followers guidance for living a moral life through its observances, beliefs, and expectations. Being virtuous and of good character are the first steps to the acquisition of 'Wisdom' in a theological sense. Theology is the wisdom which explains, defends, judges, and guides this process of character education.

Liberal education, in the Catholic tradition, can be considered as human formation appropriate to a free person. Liberal education in the Catholic sense has as its purpose to free the person so that they can think. A free person can explore, compare, accept, and reject, and liberal education aids this process aiming at freedom through understanding. However, there appears to be two dimensions to liberal education: first, enquiry and critical thinking, and second, initiating those being educated into the common culture. The latter is concerned with deepening our appreciation of the great cultural achievements, and this dominated much of the traditional curriculum of schooling. In addition, the quest for freedom in Catholic liberal education is about freedom in Christ by the cultivation of faith and reason for full human flourishing. Freedom in this sense does not merely free us from certain things but rather frees us for certain things – we are freed to live a way of life in Christ. Liberal education can also liberate students from the contingencies of their backgrounds and limited horizons on life. A Catholic liberal education aims to teach students to be good and to encourage faith, wisdom, and virtue together with shaping a balanced and integrated person so they may flourish.

Many Catholic schools have a fragmented sense of liberal education, and there has been a decline of liberal education because of the commercialisation of education. Several institutes and centres have been founded in the USA to extend the idea of a Catholic liberal education. The Institute for Catholic

Liberal Education (ICLE), which was founded in 1999, seeks to renew Catholic schools 'by drawing on the Church's tradition of education, which frees teachers and students for the joyful pursuit of faith, wisdom, and virtue'. According to the Institute, most modern schools are based on a pragmatic, utilitarian, secular philosophy that is fragmented and focused on skills, job training, and standardised tests. A Catholic liberal education, on the other hand, emphasises wisdom, independent thought, and discovery while focusing on the whole child created in the image of God. The Institute provides several resources for schools that want to adopt the Catholic classical educational philosophy. In the same way, the St. Ambrose Centre for Catholic Liberal Education and Culture exists to extend the University of Dallas' core mission – that the pursuit of wisdom, truth, and virtue is the proper and primary end of education. Individual schools have also adopted versions of a Catholic education based on this Institute and Centre. In Britain, there continues to be a discussion on liberal education with Franchi (2023a: 523) saying: 'The aspiration to human flourishing which animates the link between Catholic education and the Liberal Arts offers opportunities for dialogue on the wider aims of education'. On the continent, liberal education is often equated with the *Bildung* movement, represented by Humboldt.

John Henry Newman (1982) is often admired and cited by university and school leaders because he saw the cultivation of the intellect, engagement of the mind, as an end distinct and sufficient in itself. Later, Fr. McGucken (1943: 53) wrote that Catholic liberal education 'is a problem of synthesis of ideas, words, facts, things into unity, making them assimilable, dynamic, and alive in the individual, so that by reason of such assimilation and verification the student is transformed, lifted above his meagre environment and given an outlook over a broader horizon'. This shows a concern, as Newman did, to integrate theology with Christian liberal education which was significantly different from classical education. For Newman, liberal education was religious in the sense that a person's fulfilment lies in developing his or her proper relationship to God. In these, he followed the philosophy of the Alexandrian Fathers, such as Clement, whose ideas 'came like music to my inward ear' (Arthur and Nicholls, 2007: 121). Newman saw all knowledge as one in the unity of all that exists. However, he understood that not all education could be religious. There is a general education undertaken for the use to which it can be put, and there is another kind of education whose end lies not in some ulterior use but in the benefit, given simply by acquiring it and possessing it. This is what Newman understood by the term 'liberal education'. As he said, 'We contrast a liberal education with a commercial or a professional; yet no one can deny that commerce and the professions afford scope for the highest and most diversified powers of the mind' (Arthur and Nicholls 2007: 125).

Newman saw the value of a liberal education in the effect it should have upon the mind. He speaks of the enlargement of the mind and believed that liberal education disciplines the intellect to the 'perfection of its powers, which knows, and thinks while it knows, with the elastic force of reason'. He was concerned to emphasise that true education is the way persons live as much as how they think. A good educator, therefore, cannot be neutral about the good of the whole person under his or her charge. He also did not believe that liberal education was static or frozen in time, but he acknowledged that the canon of liberal learning could be added to. The goal of liberal education was human maturity – becoming a full human being. There have been many Catholic philosophers who agree with Newman, and Maritain (1943) summarises the purposes of education as threefold: to educate persons to cultivate their humanity, to realise their human potentialities, and to introduce them to their cultural heritage. All of this rested on a conception of human nature based on the Judeo-Christian heritage. However, essentially liberal education focuses on open-mindedness and the ability to search and analyse information critically. Liberal education is thus essentially antithetical to the 'cancel culture' that characterises some current educational institutions.

Integral education is about learning that integrates all aspects of the person: cognitive, emotional, physical, social, cultural, religious, and spiritual. It involves personal transformation and growth in order that a person can reach their potential. Integral education today is seen as a philosophy of education often linked to progressive education and is generally open to a range of philosophies. It can relate to multiple things that are innate in human beings and have an all-inclusive approach. In the Catholic tradition, it is variously referred to as 'integral development', 'integral formation', 'integral humanism', or 'integrated learning', but it is always understood that Christ is the foundation of this educational project. It is essentially an education that responds to the needs of the human person, and Pope Francis has established a Dicastery for Promoting Integral Human Development. Maritain's (1996) work on 'integral humanism' argues that true integral humanism forms persons according to an ideal and that this ideal must be connected to God. Education therefore must prepare a person for life in community according to a human ideal that embraces all that is good, true, and beautiful, including our relationship to God. He quotes Pindar, 'Learn what you are, and be such', and argues that integral education helps students to learn what they are and to become what they are, to attain their true form, and to become truly human according to the image of God; he calls it a 'human awakening'. It is a person and their full realisation by pointing out the deep realities about a human person. In the Catholic sense, this is religious.

Catholic integral education is intended to form, inform, and transform individuals through an encounter with a Christian cultural inheritance. The whole truth of this cannot be captured in one philosophy. The reality is that those in Catholic educational institutions identify differently and are educated together. Maritain (1996) recognised that such education takes place within a democracy as well as the 'pluralism' discovered in modernity, the 'autonomy of the temporal', the freedom of persons', 'the unity of social race' (meaning equality), and the impetus towards 'fraternal community'. Education is a social process, developed within a particular culture, over time, and integrates a person within that culture. Catholic educational language, however, also stresses the language of continuity with the past. So, while each human person has an essential autonomy and dignity, this is not to be understood as being independent of God.

As part of its mission to evangelise, the Catholic Church has a long history of establishing educational institutions at every level. Catholic educational institutions have consistently emphasised the need for an educational philosophy built on the foundations of a Catholic understanding of the human person. They face unique challenges as mission-driven institutions, not least being open to others. Nor can they simply have a reputation for excellence in academic achievement or community welcome or simply introduce rudimentary and incoherent elements of the Catholic faith. In 2013, the Church published *Educating to Intercultural Dialogue in Catholic School: Living in Harmony for a Civilisation of Love* which emphasises the Church's ongoing commitment to dialogue with other ways of thinking as proposed in *Gaudium et Spes* (1965). It sought to harmonise cultural and religious differences. Being open to others in Catholic educational institutions is of course an indispensable mark of catholicity, but this 'openness' cannot be seen as a conduit for religious syncretism (see Franchi, 2016). Nor can this openness to others be solely based on favourable perceptions of academic excellence.

Polyphony of Movements

In chapter 1 of the 'Instruction' (2022), education is described with the image of the 'polyphony of movements': *team movement, ecological movement, inclusive movement, and peace-making movement*, which, it is claimed, generate harmony and peace. This 'polyphony' suggests an endorsement of many guises and forms of Catholic education. The implication is that there is nothing particularly distinctive about a philosophy of Catholic education. It is worth examining in more detail this analogy of 'polyphony' in explaining what Catholic education is. Polyphony is a word that derives from the Greek word for 'many sounds'. It is divided into two types – either melodic notes that sound similar or these notes may be completely independent of each other. However, the 'Instruction' speaks also of harmony and while recognising a multiplicity of sounds (Catholic education), it suggests that these sounds combine several independent but harmonising melodies. There is not one dominant voice as each Catholic educational institution plays its own independent melodic lines.

However, all the characteristics or themes of Catholic education discussed above are interrelated and work together to produce a distinctive sound that is recognisable as Catholic. Delfra (2018) had previously used the metaphor of a musical key and concluded that

> We have chosen ... the metaphor of a musical key because it conveys this sense of how something can permeate and transform an entire activity, and yet not be requisite for it. Different musical pieces are composed in different keys. A musical key provides a coherence and unity that reverberates throughout every note of the composition. Nonetheless, there are outstanding compositions in a variety of musical keys. We find in education that "Catholic" functions much as a musical key, impacting every aspect of the endeavour and providing a coherence and unity ... We are intent on presenting a vision of education in a Catholic key that is unabashedly evangelical and ecclesial.

However, we should remember that there will be some who will rebel against the symphony and conductor by deliberately playing a wrong note – in effect exercising musical freedom in disruptive ways.

The Church needs to be able to recognise when an institution claiming to be Catholic is out of tune. Is there a polyphony of philosophies of Catholic education and how are they to be recognised and evaluated? Today, the Vatican education authorities are extremely reluctant to decide whether an officially recognised educational institution is 'Catholic' or not, even when the local bishop seeks to withdraw the title 'Catholic'. Instead, the emphasis is on unity, but not uniform practices and we are encouraged to embrace the many forms of Catholic education. In short, there are multiplicity of voices, views, and perspectives in Catholic education leading to the mission of Catholic educational institutions taking shape in many ways, including non-confessional theories of Catholic education.

There is also talk of a 'global educational pact' in the 'Instruction', an invitation that 'assumes great value for Religious Families with an educative charism that over the centuries have given birth to many educational and formation institutions' and of education in the 'culture of care' that 'is born in the family, the natural and fundamental nucleus of society, where one learns to live in relationship and in mutual respect' and extends to educational institutions in a fabric of relationships. Some of this language seems vague and open to multiple interpretations and appears to sit uneasily with the overall direction of the 'Instruction'. However, the 'Instruction' is not about choosing between either Catholic identity or openness to otherness but rather, through the dialogue with the other, is intended to stir the (re)discovery of one's own Catholic identity and while witnessing to your own Catholic faith introduce the Christian voice within the conversation. The 'Instruction' recognises that there is room for those who are not 'totally' Catholic but also acknowledges that there needs to be some defining characteristics of Catholic education. In practice, there has been a re-interpretation of the Catholic faith in contemporary culture which means that some forms of officially approved Catholic education are pluralised and detraditionalised opening the danger that these kinds of institutions will eventually become indistinct.

In summary, the missionary mandate in Matthew 28 is the reason that evangelisation is core to the Church's mission. Catechesis forms informed disciples of Christ in developmental stages to initiate and strengthen a deeper faith which also gives them a Catholic identity and a Catholic worldview. Integral education and a wider and lifelong Catholic formation in the development of faith and virtues extend this Catholic worldview and by this process helps make them more fully a human person in union with God. In each context, a liberal education will aid this process and a religious charism can strengthen it. Indeed, a philosophy of Catholic education shares many of the features of a traditional liberal education. The more explicit all these elements are, the stronger Catholic identity there will be and the more able the persons so formed will be able to freely dialogue with others of faith and non-faith. A philosophy of Catholic education does not begin from scratch, and if some think it can, then the Catholic character of education becomes obscured. Mission, identity, evangelisation, catechesis, integral education, formation in faith, and virtue as well as a liberal education aim to transform the person and the world. They are essential components of an underlying philosophy of Catholic education. What would one therefore expect to see practically in a Catholic educational institution?

Models of Catholic Education

The definitional meanings of Catholic education vary considerably, leading to Catholic institutions having numerous configurations worldwide. While many Catholic educational institutions want to be seen as 'Catholic', there is no simple way on agreeing how they should be Catholic. If we accept this, then educational models of Catholic education are essentially the philosophical foundations of any overall beliefs about learning, teaching, and curriculum content. Any educational model will be narrower than a stated philosophy and more general than the curriculum and teaching employed. However, any model must act as a guide to determine how they operate and ought to illustrate specific goals and priorities. Models also act as a framework that brings greater clarity because Catholic education as practised is a complex reality and there is a need to better understand that reality. How you view Catholic education, considering your underlying beliefs and assumptions, is often very different from how you implement those views into actual life, for example as a classroom teacher in a Catholic school. One is theory, the other is application and practice. Catholic educational institutions appear to be on a continuum from being fully religious in orientation to being fully secularised. Today, 'Catholic education' can be seen as an ambiguous term which means trying to remain Catholic is about keeping contradictions and opposites in tension. Therefore, issues of Catholic identity are repeatedly addressed and endlessly debated and critiqued.

Canon law provides a definition which appears to include catechesis, evangelisation, and religious formation, but the reality is that pragmatic definitions predominate, as context has become hugely important when interpreting the meaning of Catholic education. New models of what Catholic education means are now required to those followed traditionally, and the Vatican Dicastery for Education and Culture seeks to avoid any judgement on levels of Catholicity in Catholic institutions. Diversity is the hallmark of Catholic institutions, and context could be one that serves a predominantly Catholic community to one that serves a predominantly non-Catholic community. The Church has a long and honourable tradition of providing schools for non-Catholic communities in need of education. Therefore, approaches will differ, and much will depend on circumstances. Many models are needed to capture the diversity of Catholic education offered. As the 2022 'Instruction' from the Vatican says, 'a narrow Catholic school model is not acceptable' because 'In such schools, there is no room for those who are not 'totally' Catholic. This narrow approach, it is argued, contradicts the vision of an 'open' Catholic school with a model of a 'Church which goes forth' in dialogue with everyone'.

Morley and Piderit (2006) outline four models for Catholic higher education, but they are general enough to cover most Catholic educational institutions. The first model is the *immersion* goal which focuses on a majority Catholic institution with students, who are already actively engaged with the Catholic tradition – in other words, catechesis, evangelisation, and Catholic formation. The second model is the *persuasion* goal that seeks to give all students knowledge and an appreciation of the Catholic faith whether they are Catholic themselves – a kind of gentle persuasion. The third model is the *diaspora* goal that entails a small minority of Catholics and a focus on openness to all religious beliefs with minimal Catholic standards. The fourth model is the *cohort* goal that does not seek to generate specific Catholic knowledge or commitments in the students. In 1995, I outlined three models of Catholic education which described how the Church's religious mission was progressively distanced from its secular practice. It began with the *holistic* model that had a clear set of educational principles and policies based on Catholic teaching and a distinctive Catholic culture. The *dualistic* model simply separated out the religious dimension from the secular and substantially prepared the way for the *pluralistic* model that made no explicit appeal to Catholic teaching (Arthur, 1995: 246). There has always been a concern that Catholic institutions could lose their religious identity and become indistinguishable from their secular counterparts. Since I offered these three models in 1995, much has changed in Catholic education and there is an even greater openness to a variety of approaches to Catholic education. The pluralist model remains strong and even when much of the practice is unmistakably contrary to Catholic teaching, its defenders assure us that it is still 'Catholic'. There is a case for having a

Catholic 'presence' in Catholic schools that do not evangelise in traditional ways because of local regulations and laws – but these kinds of schools are rare. Catholic schools that simply pre-evangelise by teaching about Christianity are more common as are dualistic Catholic schools that separate catechesis from the education philosophy of the school. Holistic Catholic schools are facing multiple challenges in their attempt to integrate the Catholic faith into the whole educational philosophy of the school. What is absent is any method to determine the Catholic authenticity of these approaches.

Garcia-Huidobro (2017: 69–70) found that there were four different perspectives or stances underlying the literature on Catholic education. First, *Identity-focused*. This stance assumed that Catholic schools' main goal was the preservation of Catholicism, based upon the idea that modernity is undermining Catholic faith and culture. Second, the *Dialogical*. This perspective supposed that Catholic schools were part of the Church's cultural and religious dialogue within the world, so they should both have an explicit Catholic identity and be open to share and learn from other traditions. From this perspective, academic excellence expressed Catholic identity, but there was also a tension between the Catholic and the secular-market rationales for academic excellence. Third, the *Open*. This standpoint also assumed that Catholic schools were part of the Church's cultural and religious dialogue within the world, so they should be open to share and learn from other traditions. However, there was less clarity about the tensions between Catholic values and beliefs and the current secular, capitalist economic forces. Fourth, the *Secular*. This stance presumed that Catholic identity was mostly a private matter. Thus, Catholic schools were understood as if they were public schools with Religious Education as an added subject, having two largely disconnected curriculum goals: being excellent in secular matters and giving solid Catholic education.

Some believe that Catholic schools are not simply for Catholics but for everyone – all are welcome. Indeed, many non-Catholic parents send their children to Catholic schools. Many Catholic schools in turn respect the faith and freedom of other believers. Tony Gallagher (2004) in seeking to establish the heart of Catholic education in diverse societies offers four dimensions. Catholic schools' educators must: (1) Encourage a sense of belonging, that is students must feel welcome in the school community; (2) Provide a sense of the 'ultimate', that is students must be able to explore and reflect upon the important question of life; (3) Listen to the students own stories and their own journey of faith 'without judgement or criticism'; (4) Attend to their students' moral and social development with an emphasis on 'doing' that is encouraging service, both within the school and the community'. This model of Catholic education is perhaps one of the most common, but it makes little reference to the teaching Church. This model also appears to incorporate Karl Rahner's thesis of 'Anonymous Christianity' in that students who non-culpably fail to believe in the revelation taught by the Church can nevertheless possess saving grace. It suggests that non-believers have implicit faith and makes the understanding of what Catholic education goals are more complicated.

It is interesting to return to the Brothers of the Christian Schools and particularly their Rule (revised 2015) which explicitly states in section 17.2 that Catholic education is intended:

> To enable baptized persons to live as Christians and become disciples of Jesus Christ, the Brothers accompany them as they seek to grow in faith, fraternity, and service. They help them develop a personal relationship with God; to make their contact with his Word, the liturgy, and the sacraments a life-giving one; and to prepare themselves for social commitment.

It states that 'The life and the educational activity of the Brothers are an integral part of the Church's work of evangelization. They believe that catechesis, as the Founder insisted, is "their principal function." However, in pluralist contexts the Rule states

> In their contact with people with different religious traditions, or in highly pluralistic or secularized countries, the Brothers seek inventive ways to announce the Gospel; the witness of a Christian presence and fraternal relations, gratuitous service, the experience of prayer in common, inter- religious dialogue, and sharing with one another the story of Jesus Christ. In their turn, the Brothers allow themselves to be questioned by these people. When they work with Partners with different beliefs and religious traditions, the Brothers seek to establish common ground for cooperation based on the promotion of human dignity, solidarity among all human beings, and the integral development of the individual, in line with the Lasallian tradition.

Context is crucial here as the Brothers sometimes operate in areas where any form of evangelisation is illegal and where there is a minimal Catholic presence. The danger, however, is that the Brothers simply provide a more affordable quality education.

The Common Good Model

There is, what I call, a 'common good' model of Catholic education that is advocated by several educators. The first is by Fr. Mario D'Souza (2016) in his 'A Catholic Philosophy of Education' and another by Anthony Bryk, Valierie Lee, and Peter Holland in their 'Catholic Schools and the Common Good'. While neither name their model or philosophy as the 'common good', they do describe a model of Catholic education that could easily be called a model of the 'common good'. This model borrows much of the language from secular philosophies of education and in many ways is radical in approach. Nevertheless, both make explicit references to moral and religious values in describing the goals of Catholic education. Both texts support the idea that Catholic educational institutions ought to be committed to certain values in their mission statements whether it be personal formation or promotion of the common good.

D'Souza's (2016: 215) model begins with:

> My approach to a Catholic philosophy of education is coloured by my experience of attending a Catholic school, but it is also shaped by my continued appreciation of why there are now many approaches and formulations of Catholic philosophy of education.

D'Souza attended a Catholic school in Pakistan which had a majority of Muslim students. He believes that the plurality and diversity of his schooling produced an expansive understanding of what it means to be human and a desire to be of service to the world – to promote the common good. His approach is characterised by radical openness to education and that Catholic philosophies of education ought to be 'sensitive to local, national, and continental particularities'. Therefore, 'philosophy of education is understood as the application of the Church's universal teachings on education to particular local, cultural, and historical contexts'. He speaks of different regional philosophies of Catholic education and believes that how the Church has understood philosophy and education has never been unified or uniform. This is a rather indiscriminate formulae that virtually everyone should accept. He asserts that this model of education is revolutionary whether intended or not because its aim is to transform society.

The model he outlines is essentially a social model that emphasises the social nature of diversity and plurality in education. He employs two Thomists, Maritain and Lonergan, to support his understanding of Catholic anthropology as well as a careful, but selective, reading of the Vatican's documents on Catholic education since Vatican II. Students are to be humanised in Catholic schools, Catholic culture is to be offered to all, students are to study and grow together, differences are not to be used to separate students, and any attempt to define the school's mission in religious terms alone is seen as being too narrow. D'Souza (2016: 221) says,

> the intellectual mandate of the Catholic school must serve in showing why its worldview and anthropology are essentially unifying: it offers a unity that is based on the student as one who seeks to know, understand, and choose, and this transcends religious and cultural distinctions.

There are many who endorse such a model such as Bergman (2011) who believes that this 'social learning' is what Catholic education is and the end is a hunger and thirst for justice.

D'Souza's model is open-ended and heuristic with Catholic schools viewed as providing a kind of social service to society. He rejects traditionalist conceptions of Catholic education as simply holding on to a golden age and idealised past and consequently condemns 'inward looking Catholic education for Catholics'. Above all, he advocates that his model is suitable in 'multicultural' Europe and America claiming that the model in Pakistan was years ahead of its time. The question is whether this model is too utopian and not sustainable over the long term as the religious vision, to say nothing of the resources, that motivates and maintains it become increasingly blurred and even non-existent. He believes totally in the goodness of pluralism and diversity and in freedom being the end of education. It says little about evangelisation or catechesis but rather focuses on Catholic schools recognising and protecting the alternative faiths of their students. Indeed, he says that Catholic schools are not suitable places for evangelisation. The importance of promoting the common good of all is the chief goal of this model.

Bryk et al. (1995) offers a sketch in their Preface of how St. Madeline's Academy, Los Angeles, founded in 1889, gradually changes and by the 1980s is transformed into a school that promotes social justice. The school for most of its first 100 years is staffed by nuns who establish a traditional Catholic ethos and curriculum for a homogeneous population of white Catholic girls. Religion plays a preeminent role, and the ethos is almost monastic in tone. By the 1980s, the school is serving a largely black population who are diverse in their beliefs. Bryk et al. (1995: 10) claim that the school is now more open, friendlier, and more welcoming and that the school has a caring environment and religious education classes focus more on peace, justice, and responsibility. Students are involved in discussions, and their personal responses to issues predominate in classrooms. The school's aim is now to empower young black women for their place in society. Three commitments represent the school: '(1) an unwavering commitment to an academic program for all students, (2) school is a caring environment, and (3) institutional ideology that directs institutional action toward social justice in an ecumenical and multicultural world'. This philosophy of education seeks to influence the kind people the students will become. The aim is to advance social justice and prepare the students for democratic society. The problem with this as a model for the Catholic school is that many non-Catholic schools share the same ideology. Catholic education has no monopoly on advancing social justice or on Catholic schools being 'caring environments'.

The social character of the human person, the dignity of all, and the pursuit of the common good are key and essential elements of Catholic social doctrine. However, the basis of this social doctrine is Christ and is therefore not complete without explicit reference to core Catholic doctrines and practices. Scanlan (2008) speaks of the radical 'Catholicity' of schools that 'affirm human dignity, promote the common good, and exhibit a preferential option for the marginalised'. However, there is no mention of faith, evangelisation, identity, or catechesis in this article or any other religious terms associated with the normative Catholic understanding of education – they are either minimised or absent. This approach can slip into a kind of 'secular theism' in which belief in God is maintained but viewed as residing in this world and not separately from it. While the approach claims to reject secularism as an ideology, the resulting interpretation of education tends towards an over emphasis on the secular elements through a re-reading of Catholic sources in education which may translate theology into a secular discourse.

The danger is that a view of human nature divorced from God is the result by employing a semi-secularised Christian anthropology that has the effect of secularising the imagination of those we teach. The Church is not a political party or humanitarian organisation. Social doctrine without evangelisation, for example, in education means that in the future there will be fewer disciples of Christ, and many students will not know Christ far less understand the theological basis of the Church's distinctive social doctrine. There appears to be a need among some Catholic educationalists to articulate an explicitly Catholic vision of education and human life without excluding non-Catholics. What they do not concern themselves with is an equal interest in the 'lapsed', 'nominal', 'fallen away', 'non-practising', or 'bad' Catholics. Such themes are almost never the focus of their work, and yet Catholic education must and has a duty to invest in the student's Catholicity whether they are poor or not.

Returning to the idea of models of Catholic education, it is worth outlining the two ends of the continuum. The first is the traditional model which aims to teach students to be religious in a particular way. The model emphasises the missionary, prophetic, and evangelistic elements of the teaching Church. Such an institution would have as a minimum, a critical mass of Catholics, if not the majority who share the same faith and beliefs, who engage in common worship and prayer and celebrate the sacraments, and who would have a clear Catholic identity and be generally loyal to the institutional Church. The curriculum would be intellectually challenging with theology and philosophy recognised as central, and there would be a focus on evangelisation, catechesis, and religious formation with all three being at the core. Students would be immersed in these shared beliefs, language, symbols, liturgy, and activities of the Catholic tradition. The second is the open or pluralist model that aims to teach students about religion. The Catholic tradition is presented as one option among others, and wisdom can be sought outside of it. This open model presupposes a broader context and emphasises sharing, dialogue, discernment, democracy, student voice, ecumenism, social change, social justice, freedom, personal growth, and fulfilment and is concerned with students being socially conscious. Overall, it is pluralist in orientation and welcomes all. Between these models, there are many other variations in the continuum.

Models, of course, do not operate in isolation, and the Church is increasingly under pressure to be relevant in the present time, so models need to adapt and change since they will in practice have strengths and weaknesses. The traditional model has come under disapproval from some Catholics and secular authorities. The model is variously labelled passive, rigid, overly

Charisms, Definitions, and Models of Catholic Education 51

authoritarian, ghettoised, too triumphalist, doctrinaire, isolated, sectarian, and exclusive. The open model also faces accusations that it sees the Church as merely an agent for social change and welfare, that it lacks 'missionary thrust', encourages vagueness, de-emphasises essential and distinctly Catholic religious elements, and has an indeterminacy of its acknowledged commitments. Some say this model produces '*ala carte* Catholics' or 'cafeteria Catholics'. A single model has the potential to distort reality, and it is necessary to keep models of any description in perspective. It is believed that both models may potentially produce active and responsible disciples who seek to advance and become the best human beings they can be. Both have a formative human approach, the first through explicit faith formation by deepening the initial conversion to faith while the latter focusing more on human formation as the basis for all we do as human beings, cultivating emotional and personal maturity as a preparation for spiritual formation – you might say a form of pre-evangelisation or even more positively re-evangelisation. However, the Church's distinctive call is not a generic invitation to human fellowship but is rather more directive and is a call that is addressed to everyone: meet Jesus and welcome his Gospel, which is what John Paul II called the 'New Evangelisation'.

The taxonomies highlighted in this chapter indicate that the characteristics of mission-driven Catholic schools have some similarities and some differences. One group speaks of a socially orientated Catholicism and persons-in-community and human dignity in diversity. The other group speaks of the centrality of Christ, the need for salvation, and the sacramental or theological basis of a Catholic philosophy of education (see Geusau and Booth, 2013). John Sullivan (2001) observed that the apparent inclusiveness offered by the first group is not sufficiently related to Catholic teaching. Sullivan would recognise that the Catholic identity in schools that serve non-Catholic communities is inevitably different from Catholic identity in schools serving Catholic communities. In addition, some elements of school identity and culture might be compromised if the surrounding community is significantly different from the culture the school serves. Vatican II's *Declaration on Christian Education* (1965) states that 'all men of every race, condition and age, since they enjoy the dignity of a human being, have an inalienable right to an education'. The Declaration emphasises inclusion of the poor and the marginalised in society, but more contemporary notions of inclusion point to more radical understandings of gender, ethnicity, religious beliefs, and other differences. Sullivan (2001: 25) recognises the tensions inherent in inclusive Catholic education but ambitiously sets out 'to articulate the tension between two particular, apparently contrasting imperatives within Catholic education and then suggest a way to reduce, if not entirely to resolve, the tension between them'. These two polarities relate to two opposing viewpoints from *The Ebbing Tide* (Arthur, 1995) and *Catholic Schools and the Common Good* (Byrk et al., 1995). Sullivan (2001: 63) sees merit in both viewpoints but argues 'that the essential principles underlying a Catholic philosophy of education constitute a mode of distinctiveness with the power to be inclusive'. However, it is difficult to understand how an openness to all through a radical inclusion can sit well with a distinctive approach – it is possible that the drive for 'inclusion' itself becomes the distinctive approach. Note paragraph 85 of the Congregation for Catholic Education's publication, *The Catholic School* (1977): 'In the certainty that the Spirit is at work in every person, the Catholic School offers itself to all, non-Christians included, with all its distinctive aims and means acknowledging and promoting the spiritual and moral qualities of different civilizations'.

The authors of the models described in this chapter see differently through their models, and the challenge is not to dismiss any amount of seeing differently as inauthentic, or an exercise in bad faith, but simply to be able to account for them in terms of different lived experiences of the Catholic faith. However, not all models are equally valid, so we need to evaluate their quality and suitability by some criteria. Multiple models give Catholic schools options and a degree of flexibility to meet their circumstances, but there are some constants, not least that the Catholic faith must illuminate any philosophy of Catholic education. This means a focus on both the natural and supernatural ends of Catholic education. The criteria I recommend is the five marks of a Catholic school outlined by Archbishop Michael Miller (2006), former Secretary of the Vatican's Congregation for Catholic Education. He identified five 'essential marks' that make up a school genuinely Catholic. They are as follows: (1) inspired by a supernatural vision, (2) founded in a Christian anthropology, (3) animated by communion and community, (4) imbued with a Catholic worldview throughout the curriculum, and (5) sustained by Gospel witness. No doubt many of the models discussed would claim to meet the Miller's criteria, but it is a useful start to assess the strengths and weaknesses of each model.

The final point in this chapter concerns who attends these Catholic schools. In Latin America, 9 million students attend Catholic educational institutions from nursery to secondary schools (Woden, 2019). These Catholic institutions represent less than 7% of all school places in Latin America. Despite the rhetoric of a preferential option for the poor and the promotion of social justice, most of these schools are fee-paying and effectively exclude the poor. In Europe, only around 8 million students attend Catholic schools that are often State subsidised, but there are also socially elite private Catholic schools that parallel these State-subsidised schools. In both Europe and Latin America, all Catholic schools are generally open to non-Catholics. This raises questions about how serious the idea of the religiously motivated 'common good' school is. In Africa and Asia, we see the largest numbers of students in Catholic schools with over 40 million students attending them and there is a greater effort in offering the poor an education. In each context, a different model of Catholic education may be required.

Conclusion

The goals of Catholic education outlined in each of the models described could be said to be incomplete. We have a generic kind of model that places emphasis on academic attainment with a general philosophy that is concerned with effectiveness in education. This model is largely secular in orientation and focuses on the 'school' part of the 'Catholic school'. Second, we have a kind of model that places emphasis on the social dimensions with a philosophy open to more radical and political interpretations of education. This model seeks to transform individuals to promote the common good of society and social justice. Third, we have a kind of religious model that places emphasis on the Christian elements of education with a philosophy that is inspired by a distinctive Catholic theological approach. The model seeks to turn out believing and practising Catholics who are well educated in the faith. All three models have essential elements of what could be constructed as a philosophy of Catholic education, but none are complete in themselves. A philosophy of Catholic education needs to address the intellectual element and provide an excellent education by any standards. It needs to be concerned with the social teaching of the Church in terms of the outcomes of a Catholic education, but it essentially must address the Christian goals of education which incorporate explicit evangelisation and catechesis. However, it must be recognised that in some contexts, it is not possible to operate all three dimensions within these three models of Catholic education even when Catholic schools are established in such contexts. Government legislation can prohibit explicit evangelisation limiting the role of Catholic education to solely promoting academic attainment. Equally, assertive secular or alternative religious philosophies of education can prohibit any attempts at dialogue and exert influence on how Catholic education is provided in both theory and practice. What might be considered the constants of Catholic education are often compromised by the context making it difficult to evaluate what makes a Catholic educational institution Catholic.

Invoking the 'common good' as the signature feature of a Catholic school is problematic and incomplete as a philosophy of Catholic education. It tends to be accompanied by an approach that permits multiple worldviews, often secularised and political, into the Catholic institution and thereby the institution becomes 'pluralised' – it adapts to secular society. Catholic schools end up not knowing who they are and what they are about other than on ideological terms. One could even be said that the result of this pluralisation is that there is nothing Catholic about anything other than one's personal faith and the only tradition passed on is the one the student chooses to adopt. While there is no 'single' way of doing Catholic education, it is important that Catholic institutions do not abandon tradition for a contemporary incomplete trend. Not all manifestations of Catholic education look alike or embody the same ideas, but an eclectic approach is much like not having a distinctive philosophy. A coherent philosophy of Catholic education provides consistency in both theory and practice. Paddy Walsh (2018) argues that a philosophy of Catholic education needs to engage with the concrete reality of practice as well as the lived experience of Catholics in education. He rightly argues that Catholic education needs to answer contemporary concerns and will be part theological as well as philosophical. It is along these lines that further reflection is needed if Catholic educational institutions are not to become more secular than Catholic.

3 The Legacy of Thomism in Education

The legacy of Thomism in Catholic education persists today. Indeed, there is much in Catholic theology that depends on Thomistic terminology and there are still new scholarly resources and studies on the philosophy of Catholic education that continue to appear. However, I recognise that the very idea of a Thomistic philosophy of education will fill some with trepidation. Some view any attempt to renew a Thomist philosophy of education as a backward step and an obstacle to the Church's engagement with the contemporary world of education. They claim that Thomistic ideas in education are out of date and cannot therefore appeal to modern educators. They say that Thomism is a closed system and employs authority as its first criterion – meaning it is about pre-determined conclusions used by ecclesiastical authority. They claim that Thomism is merely a historical period in the Church's history. Interestingly, the question of whether these Thomist ideas are true or false is not addressed. If they are true, then the issue is not with the ideas but with the individuals who close their minds to these ideas. If the Thomist ideas are false, then the issue is that they are false, not that they are out of date. Some appear to have lost confidence in the search for truth and instead focus on reductionist and utilitarian ways forward. Our task here is to examine whether and how a philosopher-theologian from the Middle Ages can help in meeting the current demands of Catholic education and to show how this philosophy is open to development and that much of the criticism are simply misconceptions. Indeed, many of these critics suffer a strong historical amnesia with a partiality for false memories. Even scholars promoting the recent revival of Aristotelianism within theories of moral development and moral education often close their eyes to value that Aquinas added to those ideas.

Thomas Aquinas was born in Italy around 1225 and received his early education at the Benedictine monastery of Monte Cassino. He then studied philosophy and theology at the University of Naples before entering the Dominican Order and being ordained a priest. Thomas was a theologian and teacher who significantly influenced Western thought with his two great written works: *Summa Contra Gentiles* and the *Summa Theologiae*. The latter he wrote out of his dissatisfaction with the teaching methods of the time. The writings of Thomas are a striking work of synthesis that attempt to reconcile faith and reason in an inclusive vision. Thomas attempted to explain how everything fits together and had an openness to truth wherever it is found. He sought to make sense of the world by articulating the relationship between the divine and the human by stressing unity, integration, and wholeness. In this initiative, Thomas followed his teacher, Albert the Great, who began the process of integrating all knowledge with Christianity. Thomas therefore did not fear empirical science or the great Arabic philosophers in pursuing this initiative. Current Thomism, in summary, is the theological and philosophical school that arose as a legacy of the work and thought of Thomas Aquinas.

In terms of philosophy, Thomas argued first that Christians need philosophy to articulate the truths of reason that overlap with the truths of revelation. Second, that philosophy could challenge the non-believer's objections to Christianity including those on the grounds of reason alone. In this sense, philosophy is a natural search for understanding. However, it is important to remember that Thomas ultimately saw education principally through a theological lens, education for a life of grace leading to the glory of heaven.

Thomas, like Aristotle, was a teacher who spent a great deal of time teaching. Both believed that it is the duty of all teachers to make themselves easily understood. They also believed that real teachers must be concerned with the truth and that they must not confuse their students. It is not, of course, easy to be concise and clear. And it is hard to get to the truth of things. Some think that learning is simply a matter of the right teaching method supplemented by the latest research. Thomas believed that learning may be initiated by a teacher but stressed that a good teacher must build his teaching on the gradual development of human nature. Teaching, for him, brings us from the truth we already know to the learning of truth hitherto unfamiliar or unknown. Teachers led their students to know what they did not know. Teaching causes students to learn the truth in whatever context this discovery applies. It takes time and patience – it is not to be rushed. The goals of education, for Thomas, are to teach us things that are worthwhile through knowledge of different subjects. Education is, for Thomas, the ability to know, understand, and think. Thomas uses the works of Aristotle to bring greater clarity and simplicity to the process of human knowledge.

Thomas discusses education within the theological and philosophical framework of his major writings. Thomas did not develop a systematic 'philosophy of education' as such, although he composed two important works on teaching: one, titled On the Teacher (*De Magistro*), is devoted to the 'theory of the educability of the human individual.' The other major discussion of teaching, Whether One Man, Can Teach Another? can be found in part 1, question 117, article 1 of his *Summa Theologiae*. Thomas in his commentary on the *Metaphysics* of Aristotle provides us with his understanding of the purpose of education – 'Now all the sciences and arts are ordered to a single thing, namely to man's perfection, which is happiness'. Here the sciences and arts make up the essentials of education and human perfection and is equated with human happiness. For Thomas, education is not mechanical but always a spiritual exercise. Thomas also opposed unquestioning appeals to authority.

Thomas was one of the first scholastic thinkers to call on every human individual to make actual use of their mind for their own benefit and for the good of society. Therefore, he sees education as having a social dimension and recognises that we continue to learn throughout life. Education advances us towards wisdom and, as Maritain claims, is about 'Becoming who we are' – essentially a 'human awakening' (see Maritain, 1943). Education in this sense is a lifelong process of 'becoming'. Teaching should therefore provide the conditions for students to flourish, find the truth, and seek wisdom. It is essentially about the awakened mind. Jacques Maritain, a modern follower of Thomas, described the basic dispositions to be fostered by education: (1) love of truth, (2) love of goodness and justice, (3) simplicity and openness about existence, (4) a sense of a job well done, and (5) a sense of cooperation (see Gutek, 1997: 285).

Thomas would have said it is in our interest to desire the good life, which he argued consisted of each individual human being living a life of virtue. Only by living such a life could a person truly flourish as a human being. The 'good' in the 'good life', he argued, was common to all by virtue of their common or shared nature. The 'common good' is therefore defined in terms of the flourishing of all in society. The implication for the purposes of education is that families, schools, and universities should encourage and promote the common virtues by which all human beings ought to live if they are to flourish or realise the common good that is common to all. In sum, he appears to conclude that virtues determine who we are and the kind of world we see. Virtues are constitutive of the good life, and the goal of education is about forming people so they can live well in a world worth living in. Thomas, like Aristotle, goes to great lengths to point out what happiness is not: it is not wealth, pleasure, fame, honours, or power. Not only are these things not in themselves happiness but they also often become obstacles to true happiness because they entrap the seeker with enjoyments that are ultimately fleeting and unsatisfying.

In terms of the goals of education, Thomas begins with a definition of a human being: a human being is a rational animal and has free will, is capable of thought, and has the power of self-activity or self-determination. To this definition, he incorporates a spiritual dimension: a human being is created in the image and likeness of God, the spiritual element in human existence. That spiritual element mandates education's responsibility for spiritual formation. We are composed of both body and soul, and neither the soul nor the body is complete in itself. Unlike Aristotle, Thomas believed that natural reason is powerful but limited. He taught that theological wisdom complements and completes the philosophical wisdom of Aristotle.

Second, self-activity is the cornerstone for teaching all disciplines. According to Thomas, human beings are rational, and learning is a natural tendency. Human beings have the potential to learn, and, through understanding, the student derives meaning from things. An understanding was a natural function of the student's mind, and understanding marked the mind's activity in the process of learning. What is learned should therefore never be passively or mechanically received. Rather, it must be actively transformed into the very life of the mind by understanding. Education is futile if only memory is trained, and students regurgitate to their teachers the platitudes and the inert truths taught.

Third, education has the serious task of forming an individual: it is an integration of personality – a character guided by the ultimate ends of life. The purpose of education is to give an individual full possession of his or her powers to see, dream or imagine, conceive, judge, reason, feel, and create. Imagination enlivens knowledge. Imagination enables the student to see relationships, ask questions, and be creative. Thomas would have rejected behaviourism because it denied free will.

In summary, if we claim that education prepares human beings for life, then it follows that teachers need to ask themselves what kind of person they are seeking to promote, for it is not sensible to pursue an educational aim without considering what its concrete realisations would involve. All teachers need to be conscious of the kind of formation they offer their students since we cannot escape the fact that all education is simply the practical expression of our philosophical convictions whether articulated or not. Educating the young always involves more than simply sharing facts, it is more than merely delivering information. It's about forming the mind with a framework of meaning, teaching the difference between virtue and vice and between truth and lies. The main goal of education is therefore to help human beings more fully develop and realise their human nature.

I suggest that university education and schooling should not simply be about acquiring academic and social skills, for it is ultimately about the kind of person a student becomes. This is because humans have a purpose beyond being an instrument or tool in social processes, which is not achieved in a vacuum. To become a person, an individual needs to grow and flourish within a culture. The richer that culture, the more of a person they have a chance of becoming. The Church, families, and schools have a central purpose to educate, and the aim of education is to develop everyone as fully as possible: to make them more human.

The Thomist educational approach, as it has been developed by his disciples, has distinct philosophical and theological presuppositions, content, goals, and methods with normative commitments – many of which harking back to the ancient Greeks – that are profoundly at odds with modern culture. Fundamentally, the Thomist tradition affirms ontological and epistemological realism. Realism refers to the fact that things exist whether the human mind perceives them, but it is a philosophy that assumes that there is a real external world that can be recognised. Thomas Aquinas believed that God made it possible to acquire true knowledge so that we may know him better. The core elements of this philosophy are that knowledge is real and can be assimilated by human beings and that the senses are the doors to this knowledge. The emphasis is on experience, observation, and understanding the material world through inquiry, in a way that anticipates the later theories of educational thinkers like Locke and Dewey. Scholastic realism was endorsed by thinkers who wanted to bring together a relationship between faith (Christian theology) and reason (classical philosophy). This form of religious realism was known as perennial philosophy because of its emphasis on gaining knowledge of the abstract through the concrete. It was this enduring intellectual tradition that Pope Leo XIII was inspired by, which led him to write the encyclical *Aeternis Patris* in 1879 which promoted and revived Thomism as a major Catholic philosophy. The Pope sought to address the disarray caused by incomplete and competing worldviews. He sought to challenge modernism and set out what came to be seen as the principles of Neo-Scholasticism. A Neo-Scholasticism that is exemplified by systematic investigation, analytical precision, defined terminology, and detailed argumentation that proceeds from first principles, chief among them is that the Catholic faith is rationally justifiable. He was calling for a philosophy that offered an alternative to those current at the time.

The Response to *Aeternis Patris*

This spurred a growing movement, especially in the USA, to connect Neo-Thomism to education. Neo-Thomism came to dominate Catholic philosophy and theology in the USA in the first half of the 20th century. It exerted a particular influence on Catholic education. From 1900 onwards, education departments were established in every Catholic higher education institution which began to follow a range of Neo-Thomist conceptions of Catholic education in the context of a revival of Thomist philosophy more generally. Numerous books and articles were written by priests and laymen who worked in these Catholic universities on a philosophy of Catholic education. Pope Leo's encyclical was followed by another 'The Christian Education of Youth' (1929) by Pope Pius XI which gave greater substance to a Thomistic conception of education which is known as Neo-Thomism. These educationalists were practising philosophy of education in a Catholic context in such a way as to be compatible with Catholic doctrine and theology.

Thomas Shields was one of the earliest to advocate a Thomist conception of education at the newly created Catholic University of America in Washington DC, but he was widely seen to have done so in a modern progressive way (see Franchi (b), 2022). A laywoman, M. H. Meyer, translated and provided a commentary on Thomas's *De Magistro* in her 1929 book *The Philosophy of Teaching of St. Thomas Aquinas*. Few were trained philosophers; they were more likely to be psychologists, educationalists, or practitioners, and there was a mix of lay and clerical participants. They generally agreed on a Thomist philosophical underpinning and theological vision for education but disagreed on policies, principles, and practices. While seemingly to shun any serious engagement with the secular educational philosophies of their day, some combined progressive elements of pragmatism into their Thomist philosophies while others remained largely abstract in their approaches.

Some versions of Thomism, particularly in clerical hands, became overly legislative and disciplinary in character and perhaps caused more problems than they solved, but the versions written by these early education writers had serious worth to them. Pierre Monique (1939), for example, sought to explain the essentials of education in the light of the Christian philosophy of life in a way that showed that the Catholic conception of education was at once 'comprehensive, liberal and democratic'. Edward Fitzpatrick (1954) saw 'the purpose of education is to give an individual ... full possession of his (or her) powers to see, to dream or imagine, to conceive, to judge, to reason, to feel, to create'. Thomism in education was dynamic for them, not static. Of course, they wrote in America at a time of rampant anti-Catholicism where it was believed dogmatic Catholicism was incompatible with democracy and that it prevented Catholics from being patriotic Americans.

We need to be careful not to assume that simply because some author endorses a certain education idea it makes it 'Thomist'. The Thomist authors in education between 1900 and 1966 often disagreed among themselves. There was a genuine attempt to avoid parroting Thomas's views but rather a drive to engage with his thoughts critically. In reading their works, it is clear they provide no easy or instant answers. They reassess terminology and pursue new insights in education – this was undoubtedly not a static philosophy, but one open to discussion and debate. They wrote the following significant books that differ in the educational content and themes selected:

Thomas E. Shields (1917) *Philosophy of Education*, Washington DC, Catholic Education Press
Charles L. O'Donnell (1930) *The Philosophy of Catholic Education*
E. B. Jordan (1931) *The Philosophy of Catholic Education*
Pierre J. Monique (1939) *The Philosophy of Christian Education*
John D. Redden and Francis A. Ryan (1942) *A Catholic Philosophy of Education*
Jacques Maritain (1943) *Education at the Crossroads*
Edward A. Fitzpatrick (1953) *A Philosophy of Education*
W. J. McGucken (1943, 1950, 1954) *The Philosophy of Catholic Education*

N. G. McCluskey (1959) *Catholic Viewpoint on Education*
W. J. McGucken and M. P. Sheridan (1966) *Catholic Philosophy of Education*

These philosophies were largely understood as philosophies of school education and often ignored the wider implications of Thomism for the educative function of parents and the community. Some did not follow Thomist themes, like John Spalding (1840–1919) who as an American bishop adopted a non-Thomistic approach combining German idealism and American progressivism with some touches of Thomism into his very influential philosophy of Catholic education at the turn of the 20th century. He was educated in the Neo-Thomist tradition at the University of Louvain but was concerned that Thomism in education was sometimes vague and incomplete (Elias and Nolan, 2009: 32). He believed in open scholarship and the freedom to teach and was seen as ahead of his time. Not everyone thus followed the Neo-Thomist way, and those that did ranged from apologists to innovators in tone – they have all been well reviewed by Hunt et al. (2001). Others, like the Dominican, Thomas Donlon (1952: 18) in his *Theology of Education,* believed that 'Catholic education can claim no complete philosophy of education because no such thing exists. There is only a theology of education'. There was those who thought pursuing a strictly philosophical view of Catholic education was futile.

Neo-Thomism began to decline in the late 1950s as educators broadened their outlook to include other philosophical positions believing that the philosophy of Aristotle was outdated. By the 1960s, Thomism in education almost came to a dramatic end as well as discussions about a distinct philosophy of Catholic education. Nothing seems to have taken its place, but Catholic philosophers of education continued to write, such as John Elias publishing *Philosophy of Education: Classical and Contemporary* in 1995 which did not ignore theology in education, but he also did not promote it. A Thomist concern with a philosophy of Catholic education did not resurface until the 21st century, although Thomistic references in Catholic education did not come to a complete standstill. Neo-Thomism was charged with presenting a universal culture based solely on the elitist classicist culture of Greece and Rome.

Nevertheless, there have been many recent books that have touched on trying to resurrect interest in a philosophy of Catholic education, but only two have explicitly attempted a systematic approach aided by Neo-Thomism. They are C. L. Hancock (2017) *Recovering a Catholic Philosophy of Elementary Education* and M. O. D'Souza (2016) more progressive *A Catholic Philosophy of Education: The Church and Two Philosophers.* In addition, Gerald McCool (2000) has sought to revive *Thomism in Education* recognising that there is a crisis because of our inability to define and defend the basic purpose of a Catholic education. He believed that a new model of philosophical theology was needed for Catholic education but feared it would likely be in radical discontinuity with the past. After providing some positive alternatives to combat Catholic education losing its identity, McCool (2000: 229) says,

> At the moment, Catholic philosophers and theologians are divided over which of these alternatives represents the sound Catholic option for the future. Hence the crisis in the Catholic philosophy and theology of education and the malaise in Catholic education which it has provoked.

Today it is unusual for those preparing to teach in a Catholic school to receive any Catholic philosophy whatsoever. McCool (2000: 48) is left pessimistic as he says modern philosophers 'Question whether any philosophy, even aided by theology, can validate a worldview .... The vastness of the universe, the limited nature uncertainty of human knowledge, the partial and historical character of every viewpoint make any universal worldview philosophically impossible'. There is no unifying philosophy of Catholic education.

The first wave of the philosophy of Catholic education interest was stimulated by several contextual concerns and issues in the USA. First, there was the need to defend Catholic educational institutions in a hostile environment that was anti-Catholic. To be anti-Catholic was to be on the side of progress; however, one defined progress. Second, there was the perceived need to gain recognition for Thomism as a legitimate field of inquiry in education circles. It was in answer to these two issues together with papal encouragement that led to a Catholic philosophy of education being born. American Catholics wanted to integrate into the surrounding culture. But they also wanted to retain their difference, especially in schooling. A kind of progressive pragmatism in education was dominant at the time, and this philosophy rejected transcendence and only saw the worth of religion in its consequences. Catholicism rejected this progressive philosophy as it did not address the spiritual nature of the person.

Documents from the Congregation for Catholic Education have continued to echo, at least in a fragmented way, Thomist themes but without pronounced or distinctive philosophical expression. They are parts of the Catholic tradition, but the Vatican is non-explicit about these Thomist influences. These include the following:

1 The integral formation of the human person
2 The unity of knowledge
3 The liberation of the mind
4 The strengthening of the will
5 The social nature of human existence

There are many serious concerns and problems in schools and Universities, and many of them are in some way inter-connected. But one of the most serious flaws, and perhaps the root cause for many of the others, from a Thomistic perspective, is that the present approach to education is largely based on an instrumental-rationalist and materialistic view of the individual, life, and society. Education has been reduced to teaching and technique with aims concerned almost entirely with social efficiency. In this instrumental world of educational practice, even raising questions suggests that one supports inefficiency and lack of accountability. Because of this dominant mechanical view of education, school and university education are often perceived as a means for social success and a doorway to socio-economic upward mobility. I believe a larger framework and a much wider and deeper purpose for education is needed. I propose that an Aristotelian-Thomist framework may provide this deeper purpose for education. Both Aristotle and Thomas provide us with a philosophy grounded in common sense and intellectual insight. Both of their philosophies are open to all questions and are not closed doctrinal systems – they are not dead philosophies but rather are important keys to unlocking the answers to some of our problems today. Thomas has a balanced approach and a rich view of the human person to offer us.

Implications

What are the implications for Christian education? For many, Christian education has been on the one hand too nebulous and vague or, on the other hand, overly authoritative. When nebulous, it can have the extremely vague goal of simply 'growing closer to God', or 'God is love', or 'God is Good'. While statements like these are not wrong, failing to dig deeper into them with follow-up questions like 'Why is God good?' 'How is God good?' or 'What does 'good' mean?' does a gross injustice to their richness and depth. By using our talents to learn more about our world, we, in turn, learn more about God and our relationship with God. Thomas believed firmly that both faith and reason ultimately come from God and that the two work in collaboration. You can never make the Christian by merely learning the words of catechisms or repeating theological formulas.

Today, everything seems to be stacked against developing a philosophy of Catholic education. Many academics as well as Catholic revisionists find Catholicism unsuited to modernity and view the very idea of a Catholic philosophy, especially *a* philosophy of Catholic education, as anathema. In contrast, many other Catholics seek a distinctively Catholic systematic account of the nature and role of education that is consistent with the Catholic faith – so, it is a pluralism with certain conditions and limits chief of which is a rejection of relativism. Many Catholic philosophers of education in the 20th century, as we have noted, while showing a unity and consistency in their fundamental Catholic principles, differed substantially on the practical implications of their philosophies. As Vivian Boland (2012) notes,

> The relevance of Thomas Aquinas to Catholic education today is found in the kind of humanism he represents. At a time when there is significant fear and misunderstanding about 'faith schools', Thomas reminds us of what true humanism involves .... Where wisdom, truth, and freedom are sought as the goals of education, an appropriate understanding of the human person is required. Such an anthropology will recognise that human flourishing is found not just in technical skill and procedural expertise, but in knowledge understood more deeply, in understanding with all the resonances the term carries, and in wisdom as spiritual and contemplative activity.

In the same way Maritain observes,

> Thomism is not a museum piece .... It is relevant to every epoch. It answers modern problems, both theoretical and practical. In the face of contemporary aspirations and perplexities, it displays a power to fashion and emancipate the mind .... It is our duty to grasp the reality and the requirements of such a philosophy.

Maritain is arguing that educationalist have failed to understand the progressive nature of Thomism because of their excessive individualism. In summary, Elias (1999: 106–09) provides us with a list of points of how Thomism can help contemporary education, including Catholic education: (1) its rich view of the human person, (2) its recognition of the religious orientation of the human person, (3) its depth of social concern, (4) its liberal arts curriculum, (5) its aim to liberate the human spirit, (6) its concern for transmitting truths, and (7) its stress on the teacher and a pedagogy that is centred on the learner as a person. This kind of Neo-Scholastic philosophy sees the human person as free and relational and not static or constrained by blind obedience.

Conclusion

Despite the increasing interest in Thomism within mainstream philosophy since the Second World War, this interest has not fully percolated down to the sub-branch of educational philosophy. This is even more unfortunate and inexplicable, given the renaissance of Aristotelian philosophy within moral education. The interest in Thomas and Aristotle has thus often run-on parallel tracks, without any significant interaction for the benefit of education and schooling. I believe this has been to the detriment of both Catholic and secular philosophy of education. As Elias (1999) observes,

> Neo-Thomists made a clear distinction between the primary aim of education – an aim with a supernatural dimension, which is the formation of the person as a spiritual being – and secondary aims such as the transmission of a heritage or a culture, preparation for life in society and good citizenship, and training for family life (aims often presented as primary by progressive or pragmatic educators). Neo-Thomists asserted that the primary aim remains the same in all cultures and societies while the secondary aims change according to society's needs.
> (Maritain, 1962, 64)

Thomism's emphasis on the importance of reason and faith is central to developing a philosophy of Catholic education with its emphasis on teaching students to think critically and to understand the importance of faith in their lives. John Paul II in his *Address on the Perennial Philosophy of St. Thomas for the Youth of Our Times*, at the Angelicum University, Rome, in 1979 observed,

> The philosophy of St. Thomas deserves to be attentively studied and accepted with conviction by the youth of our day, by reason of its spirit of openness and of universalism, characteristics which are hard to find in many trends of contemporary thought.

In summary, we have seen how Thomism is marked by a strong reliance on the philosophy of Aristotle and hence a confidence in the power of reason to know and understand reality. It is these guiding principles that can help us with the theoretical foundations of a contemporary philosophy of Catholic education. It can provide a common vocabulary together with a unifying role not by dominating discussion but rather when it is blended with some other philosophies that are compatible with Catholicism. I am arguing that Thomism can provide a structure rather than a straightforward alternative to contemporary philosophies of education. For example, along the lines of the Vatican's new document on the training of priests, which calls for priests to be trained in both perennial philosophy (unmistakably a reference to Aristotelian-Thomist philosophy) as well as contemporary philosophies. There is a radical discontinuity between many forms of contemporary Catholic education and Thomas's teachings because contemporary philosophies of Catholic education share many difficulties inherited from their location in the culture of advanced modernity. We ought therefore to put Thomas's teachings in dialogue with contemporary Catholic education.

4 Philosophies and Ideologies of Catholic Education

This chapter will explore some philosophical positions that accord best with Catholic positions in education. These include perennialism, idealism, realism, and Christian existentialism (see Adler (1984), Butler (1966), Strain (1975), Broudy (1961), and Vanderberg (1983), all of which can potentially produce framed insights supportive of Catholic faith. We can look at the advantages and some of the disadvantages of each of these philosophies. The chapter will also explore the different kinds of philosophies which are largely incompatible with Catholic education if not outright hostile. A full exposition of these philosophies is not possible in this short volume, but a short introduction gives us the beginnings of a discussion. I am also not considering all philosophies but only those that have already been having influence in philosophy of education. I am here concerned with making clear Catholic educations' difference from the culture of modernity.

We have noted that the theological-philosophical foundations of Catholicism may allow for numerous options in education but that there are bounds with which the direction of this education must be retained. Not all positions are equally valid. Accepting that a narrow philosophy of Catholic schooling is unacceptable, we should explore how we can arrive at a more expanded vision and rationale for Catholic education. Catholic approaches can include some of the assumptions of existing philosophies but without endorsing some of their secular presuppositions. However, it is the case that selective appropriation of elements of any philosophies may be at odds with that philosophy's goals.

Thomas Woods (2008: 156) observes,

> Thus in a society and an age tending more and more toward secular creeds, man-cantered morality, toleration, pluralism, and emancipation from the dogmas of the past, Catholics clung to their Church's traditional exclusivity, insisting with one voice that the *only* satisfactory answer to moral chaos was that provided by the Catholic Church. It was the ultimate case of Catholic resistance to the Progressive Zeitgeist.

DOI: 10.4324/9781003486435-5

This chapter has been made available under a CC-BY-NC-ND 4.0 license.

It is interesting that Arendt (1954) commenting in 'The Crisis of Education' said that philosophy of education 'consists of an astounding hodgepodge of sense and nonsense ... under the banner of progressive education'. Catholic philosophy is a set of beliefs to live by, and it is important that any additions from other philosophical positions must to be like-minded. This sets a limit to the ontological, epistemological, and methodological commitments that those 'like-minded' philosophies can endorse.

We have seen that there was a revival of Thomism in the first half of the 20th century, but there was also a revival of Aristotelianism, Neo-Scholasticism, Platonism, and Humanism in both ecclesiastical and secular forms. This revival went under the name of perennial philosophy. Perennial philosophy is rooted in idealism and realism with the focus on knowledge that is perennial – ideas that endure through time and space. It was born in the 20th century as a reaction against progressivism (e.g., in Dewey's early works, although he later mitigated many of his progressive tenets). The followers believed that progressives in education were essentially instrumentalists and pragmatists while progressives saw perennialism as reviving absolutism. Both ended up in warring camps. With perennialism, students will acquire an understanding about the great ideas of Western civilisation. In this philosophy, the intention is that human beings will be taught to be rational and helped to develop their minds with the cultivation of the intellect as the main goal.

Idealism is one of the oldest philosophies of education and teaches that ideas are the only true reality and that truth and virtues are absolute and universal. In education, it teaches that students should be helped to appreciate broad and enduring ideas and principles. The school or university is seen as an academic place to explore and discover truth. Teaching is focused on interdisciplinary approaches with an emphasis on abstract principles and holistic learning, and the aim is to help students see the ideas that underpin reality. The great works in literature, history, and philosophy are valued and taught. Students are encouraged to have a passion for learning, and teachers are respected as authorities. Teachers employ the Socratic method for the purpose of stimulating the student's awareness of ideas with the teacher asking leading questions. There is much here that is compatible with a philosophy of Catholic education. Ultimately, idealism focuses on the role of ideas in the interpretation of existence.

Another philosophy that has strong elements that can be compatible with a philosophy of Catholic education is realism. Realism teaches that reality is to be found in the physical world that we live in and that knowledge is gained through reason and experience. Schools and universities are seen as academic institutions that promote reasoning and experimentation. The function of schools is to train and prepare students for professional life in a society where professionalism and technical skills are highly valued. The curriculum is systematic, organised, and classified under different subject-matter disciplines such as languages, mathematics, and science. While all students at the elementary level should learn the basic skills of reading, writing, arithmetic, and moral values, they should subsequently specialise in various areas of study. Higher ability students should, according to this approach, be given a liberal education in the arts and sciences, while weaker students should be channelled to vocational training. Preferring theory to practice, realists rate the study of theoretical subjects in liberal education higher than practical subjects in technical and vocational training (Ornstein and Levine, 2003). Assessment includes various types of diagnostics, competency, and achievement tests for both students and teachers.

While realism has been credited with promoting a down-to-earth form of education that prepares students for a knowledge-based economy, it has been criticised for valuing cognitive development at the expense of other forms of development in students. The realists see teachers as experts in the various disciplines. Such a teacher knows the subject thoroughly and is skilful in explaining the content to the students and in assessing the students' understanding. Clearly defined criteria in the various subject matter are taught to students, and they are formally assessed in standardised achievement tests (Ozmon and Craver, 2003).

Christian existentialism is concerned with issues relating to how we come to terms with one's existence and the notion of being. However, some existentialists reject universal and absolute ideas and hold that reality is constructed by individuals themselves. Nevertheless, this philosophy holds that every student is a free, unique, and a sentient being with personal fears, hopes, and aspirations. Existentialists are critical of schools that overlook and suppress this individuality in students and view students as a collective and passive whole to serve the needs of society. Schools should provide a broad education with many options for students to explore, reflect on, and articulate their convictions. There is no fixed curriculum the content and pedagogy are determined by the needs and preference of the students. Existentialism has been criticised for neglecting the needs of community and society, leading to selfishness and egoism (Ozmon and Craver, 2003). The existentialist teacher is one who respects the individual freedom and choice of the student. Existentialism is not a uniform body of philosophical thought and is characterised by great divergence in thinking. Catholic education can agree with some aspects of it, for example that education should cultivate self-awareness and responsibility in students, but it cannot accept that individuals make their own values without recourse to external criteria. Idealism, realism, and Christian existentialism can come in various forms that would be incompatible with any philosophy of Catholic education. However, they can also enrich such a philosophy as the early Church Fathers and the Neo-Scholastic movement demonstrated.

Alan Vincelette (2011) argues that the Church does have a Catholic philosophy of education and outlines a series of first principles of Catholic philosophy some of which are a good basis for searching for a philosophy of Catholic education. These principles are drawn from the constant teaching of the Church and from diverse figures such as Justin Martyr, Augustine, Aquinas, Bernard of Clairvaux, Newman, Stein, as well as the catechism and numerous encyclicals. Together, these principles can help shape what an authentic philosophy of Catholic education might look like. Using some of these principles, we could begin with the inalienable dignity of the human being who, as human person, is a being that possesses intrinsic value and must be loved for its own sake. Regarding human knowledge, this originates from the senses and experience is the foundations of philosophical knowledge. While knowledge begins with experience, the intellect is actively involved in the cognitive process. The intellect can grasp the nature of reality to some degree since human beings have the capacity to know reality. Humans also possess a free will, which is a power to choose one action or another. Faith and reason harmoniously work together in the development of philosophical and theological truths. It is difficult to see how any Catholic philosophy could reject any of these claims without forfeiting their fidelity to the Catholic faith.

Secularising Philosophies of Education

Catholic education has endured in the face of crisis and secularising influences (Arthur, 2009) An awareness of these alternative philosophical perspectives on education will help Catholic educators blend some of the practical elements into their own philosophy of Catholic education. It continues to draw on the Neo-Scholastic heritage as well as blend with different philosophies. These philosophies have the task of making the faith clearer based on reason and experience. They also seek the truth on the grounds of our common humanity and life in the world. Catholic theology encounters philosophy of a particular time, culture, and schools of thought. It is why 'The Church has been justified in consistently proposing St Thomas as a master of thought and a model of the right way to pursue theology'. In education, as we have seen in Chapter 3, Thomas had already proposed many of the so-called progressive elements of education we see being advocated today.

There is also a growing conviction that the secularising of culture and education is not inconsequential, either for the health of society or for individuals. The reality is that we live in a consumer and materialistic society that continues the move towards a secular orientation – an orientation that often eliminates rival views from public education. Within academia and education more generally, there appears to be an acceptance without question of the philosophical necessity of the secular position. It was Augustine in the 4th century who floated a certain new meaning on how we came to understand the 'secular'. For Augustine, the world was divided into the secular realm and the spiritual realm. Whilst he maintained that both these realms related to each other, there nevertheless grow up a sharp distinction, at least in theory, between the secular – concerned with the affairs of the world – and the spiritual – concerned with the affairs of the next world. Augustine had increasingly differentiated between the City of God and the City of Man, the latter meaning 'the world of men and time' after the fall. Aquinas accepted the validity of the 'secular' as part of God's creation but insisted that the purpose of life transcended this world. Therefore, there was a point beyond which natural reason could not go. The origins of our current understanding of 'secular' consequently lay within the Christian religion, and the secular came to mean the opposite of sacred. This dualism became a keynote of European culture and thinking. However, it gradually acquired a negative inflection and even became the preliminary stage to doing without religion altogether.

This immersion in the secular has created the illusion that humanity can take control of itself and its own destiny – that we are totally self-sufficient. When the focus becomes exclusively systematic, the 'secular' moves to 'secularism' which is an ideology that can be read inter alia as a philosophy of education – it is philosophical secularism that rejects belief in a transcendent power. Today, there is a major re-orientation in the way people think brought about by secularism which uses the 'truth and illusion' argument – 'we are neutral, you are biased' which is used to obscure its ideological character by the appearance of balance. Religion is always considered in the exclusive secular worldview as reactionary or even fanatical. So, for instance, to his book, *God Is Not Great*, Christopher Hitchens appends the insidious subtitle *How Religion Poisons Everything*. In *The God Delusion*, Richard Dawkins asserts that teaching children religion is 'child abuse' and ought to be outlawed. In *Breaking the Spell*, Daniel C. Dennett, in the guise of studying religion objectively, dismisses religion. Sam Harris follows up his bestselling *The End of Faith* with a slim but insulting *Letter to a Christian Nation*. It must be observed, however, that none of these writers offers any alternative new philosophy of education to replace classical conceptions of either secular or religious provenance.

Many modern philosophies of education are a kind of protest type of philosophy set aside a climate of 'postmodernity' that appears to preclude easy definition. The most dominant approaches of philosophy, educational theory, and philosophy of education currently practised in the Western world represent a pronounced departure from the fundamental patterns of the Greek-Jewish-Christian tradition. John Henry Newman believed that the Church is confronted by a 'darkness different in kind from any that has been before it'. In each of these philosophical approaches, there is a tendency toward the denial of, or an indifference regarding, the existence of a Transcendent Being.

Nearly all modern theories of education either explicitly or implicitly assume that God does not exist or at least that the question of his existence does not carry any educational relevance. God is omitted from their philosophies, in contrast to Catholic interpretations of education which begin with the assumption that God exists. That is why these ideologically oppositional philosophies of education not only dilute Catholic education but can also extinguish it from within. This is because such philosophies, when adopted, are essentially political in nature and are inherently incompatible with Catholicism. They are not benign or hospitable to the aims of Catholic education, and their focus is on the immanent and temporal, not the transcendent and eternal. These would include Marxism, pragmatism, and postmodernism, all of which have given rise to or accompany even more radical versions in the form of materialism, naturalism, secularism, hedonic utilitarianism, and some forms of existentialism. Exceptions to this rule include neo-Aristotelian and analytical philosophies of education, which are grounded in ontological realism and epistemological rationalism. I would also exclude Dewey's later philosophy, as represented by his 1938 book *Education and Experience* and subsequent works. Further perspectives are dominating contemporary discussions in education, including gay and lesbian philosophy, anti-racist theory, ecological thought, and transhumanism. It is often difficult to separate these philosophies from one another particularly regarding their hermeneutical fundaments which must be taken into consideration to a larger extent than has been done so far. All of them treat human beings as indefinitely plastic and malleable with no givens. It is interesting that many students are often under the constant perception that they are being measured against these philosophies.

The idea that human beings are filled with latent goodness and can do all things through their willpower is an extreme secular manifestation of the 5th century heresy of Pelagianism. Many modern philosophies take an activist and engaged stance and use education to promote a society more egalitarian and inclusive. Yet they promote theories of social justice that are divorced from any account of the common good and equate justice with uncritical identity endorsements (Arthur et al., 2021). Many educational philosophers now place the ascendency of their preferred ideologies ahead of any commitments to free inquiry and discussion or to philosophy's disciplinary norms. Ideologies also have 'militant officers' or 'activists' who spread and develop the ideology. John O'Malley S. J. (2008) put it this way in his *Whatever Happened at Vatican II*:

> The Thinkers of the Enlightenment turned their backs on the past, turned their faces resolutely to the future, and looked forward to better things to come. Among these things was a new era of liberty, equality, and fraternity ... no more dogma, for Reason was the only god to be adored .... Modernity had become an ideology, perhaps several ideologies, all of them antagonistic in some measure to Catholicism.

Ideology purports to explain reality, but ideology is the opposite of philosophy. Ideologies may reflect some degree of reality but always fall short of the whole. As Feuer (2010: xvii) commented,

> One cannot predict an end to ideology; one can say, however, that until intellectuals cease to be profits and ideologists, and become instead men of intellect, the 'intellectuals', and their specific intellectual expression, 'ideology', will be a force increasingly hostile to the advancement of civilization.

Ideologies in education can shape policies, expectations, and outcomes, and they can convey and reinforce attitudes and values that are contrary to Catholicism. Traditional philosophies, such as idealism, realism, and Thomism, were based on a metaphysical view of reality or as Gutek (1997: 153) says,

> These philosophies, which explained reality in terms of universal being or essence, are therefore abstract in the sense that they answered the question What is real? in general, abstract, and universal terms. In contrast, ideologies are contextual and concrete. By contextual we mean that they are heavily related to time, their historical point of origin, and to place, a geographical, economic, political, sociological situation.

People find it hard to make sense of this complex world – a secular world. It has become attractive to accept simple explanations of the world. The conditions for increased ideological thinking are rife, and an inability to consider different perspectives dominates this thinking. Pope Benedict, in 1958, said,

> This so-called Christian Europe ... has become the birthplace of a new paganism, which is growing steadily in the heart of the Church and threatens to undermine her from within. The outward shape of the modern Church has become the Church of pagans and is constantly becoming even more so. She is no longer ... a Church comprised of pagans who became Christians, but a Church of pagans who still call themselves Christians, but actually have become pagans.

Henri de Lubac S. J. (1995) called it the 'The Drama of Atheistic Humanism' and 'It is not true, as sometimes said, that man cannot organise the world without God. What is true is that, without God, he can only organize it against man. Exclusive humanism is inhuman humanism'. Here de Lubac is speaking of the self-deification of man and how this produced the monstrous catastrophes of the past 200 years alone.

Different Branches of the Same Tree

Each philosophy has many branches. The dominant contemporary worldview in European education is underpinned by secularist ideologies of education. Twenty-first-century worldviews presented in most common or public schools are secular with religious worldviews often excluded, criticised, or ridiculed. It is in this context that we must understand secular education. Philosophically, the 'secular' can be considered as conceptually prior to the political doctrine of 'secularism'. However, a secular world or society is not necessarily a society without God, but it is a society without a religion in the public spaces. Nor does being secularised in every case mean or result in a hard secularism. Different manifestations and degrees of secularity may result in positive or negative views of religion. In the positive dimension, a kind of secular mentality has the theoretical potential to be 'neutral' – we all engage in secular tasks; working, eating, looking after others, and all are essential and necessary to human life – none of these require to be imbued with any explicit religious meaning. Nevertheless, the Church recognises the call to holiness in all these secular contexts and activities. Each may be understood or point to something eternal, but many people living fully secular lives do not see or feel this point.

The ideal of neutrality for secular education is something that is advocated at a philosophical level by educationalists who wish to see a neutral learning. Paradoxically, many of those 'neutralists' simultaneously argue for highly divisive subjectivist identity theories that are anything but 'neutral'. The aims of secular education became premised on the belief that there is nothing beyond the natural, the material, and the physical world – no soul, no mystery, and no supernatural. The purpose of secular education is clearly intended to socialise children into a powerful set of naturalistic political assumptions, affections, and practices. It uncritically initiates children into secular ways of thinking by using secular categories of explanation that exclude or ignore alternatives. The secular person educated within this system has no other end than their own chosen desires which renders the 'secular' synonymous with arbitrariness and informs modern consumerism and its attendant hyper-liberalism. It goes hand in hand with relativism, with the rejection of metaphysics, and the concept of truth itself. Secular education can also be informed by an ideology that privileges impersonal, deterministic forces at the expense of moral agency. It can leave the young feeling hollow and leading atomised lives. This secular education is not neutral or benign because it shows partiality to a non-religious relativistic outlook and should therefore be viewed as illiberal.

Unfortunately, members of the Church have in many places variously accommodated, resisted, or submitted to these modern secular influences on its own schools and on society. Catholic schools are not intended to be secular schools with a Catholic name or simply offer a superior secular education, but rather they are meant to offer a true alternative to the naturalist orientation of secular education models of schooling. The ground in which Catholic school systems operate continues to shift, and secular society seems to be transforming exponentially, making the preservation of a Catholic alternative to secular education difficult to maintain. The implicit purpose of secular education is to free society from religious ideas, and its influence on Catholic institutions is subtle and gradual, with the Church often unaware of it. Malcolm Muggeridge once posed the question: 'How do you boil a frog'. Well, he answered you do not boil it by dropping it into a pan of hot water – the frog would simply jump out. No, instead you place the frog in a pan of cold water and gradually raise the temperature on an incremental basis. The secularisation effect is like that – the frog will have no idea that he is being boiled until it is too late. It is a slow process of assimilating worldly assumptions. As C. S. Lewis in a 1945 essay on 'Christian Apologetics' observed, 'Emphasise only the natural fit between the gospel and the spirit of the age and we will have an easy, comfortable gospel that is closer to our age than to the gospel ....' Catholic identity would become less meaningful and more and more marginal in the public space.

It is perhaps worth reminding us of the *Address to the Young* that St Basil of Caesarea (330–379) wrote and who endorsed the usefulness of secular learning, by which he meant Greek literature, calling it 'the wisdom drawn from outside'. The first chapter in this book similarly highlighted the affinities between analytical philosophy of education, as practised at the close of the 20th century, and some fundamental aspects of Catholic philosophy. St. Basil argued that secular culture must be understood to frame a critique of it and that we need to affirm what is genuinely good in culture. However, this must be carried out from the perspective of someone who has been catechetically formed and is strong in the Christian faith. If students are not strong in the faith, then they may interpret life solely from the material world and will be immersed in a philosophy of secularism that teaches them that whatever exists can be explained by natural causes and hence denying the supernatural. The future scenario of such an education would result in the last fragments of a philosophy of Catholic education that had concerned itself with the truth and coherence of Catholic claims in education being dissolved into a variety of pursuits, lacking unity and Catholic authenticity. The answer, Holder (1992) suggests, is 'Neither naïve acceptance, nor anxious withdrawal, nor unqualified resistance is the appropriate Christian response to the culture we live in'. What is needed is an informed and judicious cultural critique of the fragmented discourse on Catholic education.

Secularism has produced many other 'isms', all representing some idea, approach, or view and most originate with a particular thinker. These philosophies increasingly acquire a somewhat wider series of meanings and became largely intertwined with a range of progressive socio-political philosophies that are not totally coherent or clearly bounded. They emerged largely in the 1960s, and their philosophical assumptions contain aims, subject matters, and methods for education. Charles Taylor (2008: 2) says we have moved from a society where belief in God is unchallenged and unproblematic to one in which it is merely one option among many others. Taylor believes that what makes this 'secularism' different from previous understandings is the fact that it is marked by an unprecedented pluralism of outlook, both religious and non-religious, in which the proportion of religious belief is smaller than ever before. Secular views of reality, truth, and ethics are contrary to God's revealed word. Taylor identifies three stages in the secularising process (1) a withdrawal of the religious worldview, (2) decline in personal religious practice and commitment, and (3) a shift in culture away from assuming religious faith is the norm.

Hauerwas (2007: 173) has observed that 'the habits that constitutes the secular imagination are so embedded in how Christian's understand the world we no longer have the ability to recognise the power they have over us'. Jürgen Habermas (2003) develops the idea of a post-secular society, partly as a response against excessive secularism. This would appear to give some space to religion, but on what terms? He argues that religious communities must 'screen' their theological presuppositions inherent in their language, and they must accept plurality, accept human rights, and communicate with reason. The way he describes this process is unfortunately tantamount to neutralising religious language and would have the effect of disengaging individuals from traditional religious communities of religious belonging and believing. Secularism and many of its offshoots have fundamentally irreconcilable definitions of the human person so Catholics ought not to be carried away by secular presuppositions.

Philosophical materialism is connected to secularism; it totally denies the existence of a soul. Matter is all there is, and the idea of the non-material is seen as a myth. In this view, a person is merely a collection of chemicals and interactions between them. We only do what the chemicals and nerves 'tell us' to do. Because human behaviour is said to be merely the result of physical interactions over which we have no control, there is no such thing as morally right or wrong nor is there free will. Secularism also seeks to interpret life based on principles solely from the material world. The argument, which is often absent and more like an unquestioned assumption, is that materialism and secularism are rational while religion is irrational. Secularism and materialism remove the things that make us human and make us more susceptible to ideology. Both spawn multiple variants that dissolve the goals and practices of Catholic education. Marxism combines both secularism and materialism. Marxism is a radical critique of capitalism, and within it, the role of education is to give the students the insight to demystify capitalism and become agents of social change – indeed Marxism demands change in the world. Marx believed that the history of civilisations was defined by class struggle – conflict theory – the teacher is thus viewed as a 'transformative intellectual'. He believed that the task of a genuine education, based on the principle of scientific socialism that he developed, required the eradication of false consciousness from the minds of the proletariat. Western education is based on exploitation and oppression: it teaches proletariat children that they exist to be dominated and that they are kept in a state of false consciousness.

Marxism

For Marxists, the functionalist idea that education fosters equal opportunities for all and that it is a fair system is a capitalist myth. It is perpetuated to persuade the working class to accept their subjugation as normal and natural and to believe that they share the same interests as the capitalist ruling class. Education under capitalism for the Marxist promotes conformity and passivity, and where there is inequality, there is oppression and exploitation. This stirs up hatred and resentment among the exploited. Students are not taught to think for themselves; they are taught to be compliant and how to serve the capitalist ruling class. Education justifies capitalism and legitimises inequalities. Meritocracy is a capitalist myth used to subdue the working class and create false consciousness. Equalisation of educational opportunity is the Marxist educational goal. Marxist education aims at maximum good to the maximum number. Social advancement is to be ensured through education. Education is considered as the greatest instrument of social change, so to escape from the chains of society, the exploited need an 'education' specifically in the ideological doctrine of Marxism (see Apple, 1979).

The role of the teacher is significant and crucial in Marxist education. He must be fully equipped not only with the content of education but also the Marxist methodology of teaching as well as Marxist aims of education. A Marxist teacher must entirely be different in attitude and temperament from a bourgeois teacher. His philosophy of teaching will be the Marxist philosophy. He must be an active member of the Marxist social order. The aims of Marxist education can be summarised as follows:

1. No discrimination will be made in respect of educational opportunities. Education is to be mandatory for all sections of the society irrespective of caste, creed, sex, and social and economic status.
2. Common education is to be provided to both men and women. Coeducation is an accepted principle in Marxism.
3. Education will be universal and compulsory.
4. No discrimination is to be made among schools. Establishment of common school system is the cherished goal of Marxism.
5. Marxism advocates secular education in schools.
6. In Marxist system of education, there will be only one agency – the state. Private agency is banned in Marxist educational administration.

It is difficult to see how Marxism and postmodernism sit with a philosophy of Catholic education – it is ultimately not possible because they are radically at odds with the fundamental characteristics of Catholic thought and practice. They are also fundamentally at odds with one another, which is a different story, as Marxists have nothing but contempt for postmodernism as a late-capitalist ideology perpetuating 'false consciousness'. The Church stands in a very different relationship with these modern philosophies than it did with those classical philosophies in the pagan past. Many modern philosophies do not recognise the transcendent, nor do they regard notions of transcendence as benign. Many Catholic educationalists fail to see these philosophies clearly, far less their implications, and at a time when they may no longer be convinced of the centuries-old Catholic values at the heart of Catholic education. The more they discuss theology of education, the less agreement there often is.

If we are to regain an understanding of the Catholic tradition in philosophy, we must realise that at the heart of the matter is the nature and the human being and the purpose and meaning of our lives. Aquinas is one of the towering figures in Western philosophy and theology, but it is important to remember that theology neither began nor ended with Aquinas; this is even more true of philosophy. Haldane argues that 'A Catholic may be a good philosopher without being a Thomist, and without practising "Catholic philosophy"; but it is worth such a person considering why they would resist the possibility of harnessing their reason to their faith'. It is also worth saying that while some Catholic philosophers will begin their philosophical work based on their faith, the discipline of philosophy does not. The Catholic faith must illuminate any philosophy of Catholic education since Catholic education devoid of faith is deprived of its defining character.

Other radical theorists follow many aspects of Marxist educational philosophy. Critical theorists, like social re-constructionists, believe that systems must be changed to overcome oppression and improve human conditions. Paulo Freire (1921–1997) was a Brazilian whose experiences living in poverty led him to champion education and literacy as the vehicle for social change. In his view, humans must learn to resist oppression and not become its victims, nor oppress others. To do so requires discussion and critical consciousness, the development of awareness to overcome domination and oppression. Rather than 'teaching as banking', in which the educator deposits information into students' heads, Freire saw teaching and learning as a process of inquiry in which the child must invent and reinvent the world. The Marxist tradition claims Freire as its own despite the overtly Catholic character of his work (see Madero, 2015). This secularising of selected academics also occurred to the radical philosophy of de-schooling society proposed by Ivan Illich, who studied under the Thomist, Jacques Maritain.

Postmodernism

Postmodernism is a philosophy/ideology hostile to Catholicism even if it has almost disappeared from contemporary discussions as a useful category for analysis. It has infiltrated people's thinking even if no one knows what it is. As a philosophy, it takes the position that knowledge in any objective sense is impossible, and nothing is stable in the world outside of the mind. Definitions are just constructs and science is reduced to fiction and is nothing more than a highly complex linguistic construct. Morality has no objective grounding and is essentially oppressive and there is no truth. For the postmodernist, reality is essentially conflict that can never be resolved or come to an end, and it rejects grand narratives, like Christianity (and indeed Marxism), and deconstructs authority which leads to our disunity. It encourages extreme scepticism, and definitions of almost everything become blurred. Philosophy is about language and the power structures they conceal and not the ultimate nature of things. Many of these philosophies adopt meta-positions vis-à-vis society and seek to change it in a revolutionary way. Opponents of Catholic education, to borrow a few words from Searle (1996: 98), 'have more energy and enthusiasm, not to say fanaticism and intolerance'.

Diez de Rio (2016) has provided a useful list of postmodern preferences that capture some of the positions that some Catholics have, often unconsciously, come to respect or even accept because of their daily immersion in postmodern influences. Some of these preferences are as follows:

The individual to the universal
Diversity to homogeneity
Multi-criteria to norms and dogma
Sentiment to reason
Syncretism to unity of belief
What is particular to what is universal
Subjectivity to objectivity
Options to obligations
Multiplicity and difference to uniqueness and uniformity
Minorities to majorities
Personalism to authority
Ambiguity to clarity and distinction
What is ephemeral, unstable, and transitory to what is firm, stable, and lasting

In short, the ontological and epistemological anti-realism driving postmodernism, with its exaltation of self-chosen identities, is more anti-thetical to Catholic philosophy than Marxism ever was, let alone the pragmatism of the early John Dewey.

Radical Implications

McDonough (2012, 2016) provides a good example of how a Catholic educationalist not only accepts much oppositional philosophy but also advocates that it should be the norm in Catholic education. McDonough believes that there is an 'overemphasis' on faith and doctrine in Catholic education and that how students experience the faith is far more important than how the institutional Church defines it. He argues that the aims of Catholic education are too narrowly defined and that this does not recognise the internal diversity within the Church as regards the interpretation of Catholic education. He proposes that there is great merit in recognising multiple Catholic identities and that contrasting Catholic education with secular philosophies of education should not be construed sharply. For McDonough, the purpose of Catholic education is to nurture dissenting voices and through this process create different kinds of Catholic identity. Catholic notions of identity can be both singular and institutional, but McDonough represents a particular brand of Catholic educationalist who dissents from traditional ideas about Catholic education and embraces different philosophies no matter how contrary they are to the essential characteristics of a philosophy of Catholic education. His proposals represent a radical theological change to the anthropological underpinnings of the Church's understanding of humanity, sexuality, gender, morality, and much more besides. For this reason, McDonough can be taken as a representative of the more radical or progressive philosophers of Catholic education, and it is therefore worth exploring further the underlying philosophical and anthropological assumptions of his thinking.

First, these radical ideas can be located within the debate over whether Catholic doctrines, which are concerned with our supernatural ends, should have an influence over Catholic education. The approach comes with a set of distinctive themes that are informed by arguments and ideas that can trace their lineage to progressive educational philosophies which began in opposition to Catholic education. Academics in education, including Catholic educationalists, are often immersed in a confusing melange of progressive philosophies that include Marxism, pragmaticism, liberalism, naturalism, secularism, and postmodernism. These oppositional philosophies to Catholicism form the wellspring of progressive thinking, and they lie behind McDonough's thinking. For example, McDonough promotes the primacy of the individual over and against the claims of any collective – in this case, the authority of the Catholic Church's teachings. Students are to run their own lives through self-authorship – no relational aspect as part of the 'people of God' is even considered by McDonough. More important for McDonough is the subjective experience and voice of the student indicating that the student should be free of any constraints on them – becoming radically autonomous individuals. Another line of his thought would appear to be that we can change and improve our understanding of Catholic education using applied reason and downplaying revelation, scripture, and doctrine. McDonough, while embracing much of these radical philosophies, is careful to say that he does not accept these powerful ideologies completely. Where does this leave him – somewhere between partial adherence to Church teaching and complete rejection of it. He certainly privileges personal experience over what the Church teaches and seeks to reground authority in the Church by restraining magisterial teaching. He seeks to encourage the student's capacity for rebellion against authority of all kinds. Such an approach does not preserve the Catholic identity of education but on the contrary results in the eventual loss of anything distinctly Catholic.

Second, a Catholic anthropology serves as a powerful tool in dialogue with those outside of the Church. The Church has taught that through reason we can presume the equality of all human beings and that as humans we are unique and are endowed with certain human rights and capacities for the good. Based on this anthropology, it is assumed that human beings are searching for meaning and purpose in this universe and through dialogue we can make common cause with other religions and secularism. There are tensions and major obstacles to this line of thought at the practical level, but more importantly, this line of thought only goes so far as it generally excludes distinctive theological tenets of the Catholic faith and is not therefore complete for a Catholic audience. However, it is argued that Catholic educational institutions are now so diverse and pluralist that the idea of them being communities of faith is no longer credible. The definitional tension arises in how can these institutions be open to others while anchored in a solid theological identity? How can they be committed to openness and dialogue without embracing cultural relativism? What has happened is that some like McDonough apply this incomplete or partial Catholic anthropology to the 'pluralist' Catholic school treating it not as an ecclesial entity but as an external body that requires internal dialogue – this view has been more explicitly promoted in a doctoral thesis at the Catholic University of Leuven (see Richards, 2019) through the idea of the 'Catholic Dialogue School'. The anthropological assumptions behind this way of thinking are a result of political-theological thought that is often held by more progressive thinkers in the Church who believe that human nature can be perfected through new insights, learning, and knowledge acquired independently of the Church. Indeed, the Catholic Dialogue School is a distinctive approach of the University of Leuven which is critical of any attempt to begin the reconfessionalisation of Catholic education.

The Leuven project on Enhancing Catholic School Identity has been influential in some Western dioceses. In a highly defensive response to the *Review of the Religious Education Curriculum for Catholic Schools in the Archdiocese of Melbourne*, Professor Didier Pollefeyt (2023) at Leuven argues that any attempt at the reconfessionalisation of Catholic schools will only serve to create further polarisation and fragmentation. He argues that pluralisation, secularisation, and detraditionalisation are phenomena seen in all Western countries and therefore 'ecclesial reconfessionalisation, applied through a compulsory neo-catechetical formation' in Catholic education, is mistaken – notice the prejudicial use of 'ecclesial' and 'neo'. He makes a bold and contentious claim that current magisterial priorities for dialogue and synodality support him and that the theologically normative positions for his approach 'are wholly consistent with the vision of Catholic education that has been articulated consistently by the Magisterium'. Two other models for Catholic religious education from the Leuven project are advocated: 'Hermeneutical Communicative Model' and the 'Pedagogy of Encounter'. Their whole approach is based and justified on the 'empirical' data he has collected indicating that students in many Catholic schools in the West are either non-practising Catholics or non-Catholics. Of course, none of this is new as Fr. Paddy Purnell S. J. came to the same conclusions and approach in his book *Our Faith Story* (1985) in the UK. Pollefeyt not only ends by calling for dialogue but also says that those who criticise his position are guilty of 'polarising argumentation' and have an ideological agenda – an interesting beginning to dialogue.

Catholic in Name-Only

A distinction ought to be made between goals and practices in education. The goal is the desired endpoint while the practice leads to the attainment of the goal. If the goals are vague and generalised, then they will not provide sufficient direction for the practices. Therefore, Catholic education's vision, goals, aims, and objectives need to serve as a compass to guide practice in education. There are opposing views about educational practices – about pedagogy that describes how teachers cultivate, nurture, sustain, and transform their students. Pedagogy can cover anything from class teaching, assessment, and classroom discipline. Now we need to ask the question whether there are educational practices that correspond to Catholic teaching? What impact does a Catholic school's philosophical stance have on practice? Is there a symbiotic relationship between a philosophy of Catholic education and particular practices in Catholic educational institutions? The first thing to note is that in terms of Catholic understandings of the human being and the aims of education, there is a huge gulf between some philosophies and a philosophy of Catholic education making them incompatible. However, there can be a sharing of common teaching methods, albeit used for different ends.

The next question is whether there is a religious dimension to learning? What is the educational content to Catholic education? How would, for example, Catholic social teaching influence what is chosen to be taught? While the Church does not espouse one particular methodology or teaching materials for transmitting Catholic education, it can draw on a rich moral, artistic, scientific, and intellectual treasury of the Catholic Church. Because the Church believes that each person is endowed with dignity and reason, it follows that teaching methods should be inspired by kindness, compassion, care, and even a friendship with the students. If none of these are embedded in the teaching methods or materials, then it ought not to be called Catholic education. Teaching students to be thoughtful and conscientious is very different from teaching them to question all manner of authority.

Albert Einstein once famously quipped: 'In theory, theory and practice are the same. In practice, they are not'. If it is Catholic education you wish to achieve, then it is the employment of certain practices that will help get you there – same practice different goals. However, practices can change the goals by diverting the educator from the ultimate telos. Practice can become the philosophy itself by emphasising, say an entirely instrumental approach which loses sight of the original reasons for providing a Catholic education. It would be like driving through a large dessert having lost your map – without a reference point, you are truly lost. There needs to be integration of philosophy with practice; otherwise, practices can undermine your philosophy of education. Progressive education, for example, can also be seen as a loose collection of practices. Consequently, while the methods of teaching may be similar or the same between progressive and perennial approaches, these methods cannot be allowed to become the outcome for their own sake. There can be tension between a philosophy of Catholic education and particular practices borrowed from incompatible philosophies which in no way presuppose God.

There are modern educational philosophies that lead to specific pedagogical recommendations for the classroom and so demonstrate a strong relationship between philosophy and practice (Dennick, 2012). However, regarding a philosophy of Catholic education, because they are often vague in expression, the relationship fits loosely together. There is a pragmatic approach of taking from each school of philosophy those elements that are found to be useful in the classroom. Therefore, Catholic teachers need to balance the philosophy of the school against their practical classroom teaching. There is also the problem of increasing government legislation and regulation, for example about standardised tests or pre-packaged curricula, that influence school practice no matter how the school understands it mission. However, as I have argued elsewhere (Arthur, 2013) despite Catholic institutions being founded upon a Catholic identity and philosophy, the actual practice frequently differs little from that in secular or alternative philosophical institutions. The integration of a philosophical stance into teaching and learning practices in Catholic institutions is a challenging issue, but the secularisation process is often a self-induced internal process, further loosening the Catholic institution from their connection with the teaching Church.

Liberal and progressive views on education often claim to see illiberal practices in Catholic institutions and yet tolerate them so long as they are not very Catholic. Unlike classical liberalism, which allowed for freedom of thought and expression, the contemporary liberal perspective emphasises critical and independent thinking, problem-solving, investigative methods, open debate, creativity and original thought, freedom of expression, and good thinking skills, and it seeks to treat students equally and with respect as valuable persons. It believes that faith institutions discourage students from thinking critically and that they stifle self-expression and the questioning of knowledge and claims that the Catholic Church is authoritarian which influences its pedagogical approaches. Liberals tend to believe that the Church destroys the life of intelligence making their institutions less free for their students. The question, however, is where is the evidence for these claims? Catholic schools have often taken on board these liberal and progressive methodologies – indeed it was the strong influence of progressive education in the 1960s that led to the pedagogy in Catholic schools changing. Producing an autonomous student who can become a good citizen in a liberal democracy is often an aim of Catholic institutions. There is nothing un-Catholic about that aim as such. The problem is the additional baggage that this aim often carries, where the ideas of such psycho-social competences are relativised and subjectivised beyond good measure.

What does this process potentially mean for Catholic education institutions? If unchecked, it will result in the use of a new language in their mission statements that is vague, which emphasises what is shared with other religions and particularly with secular society in general. The institution can now employ a humanistic vocabulary that all might agree on and make vague contextual references to religious heritage and background. Policies are constructed to ensure there is no discrimination in recruitment of staff or admissions of students. Questions should not be asked of a person's religious affiliation in interviews. The process has gone from being 'committed' to being 'sympathetic' to 'familiar' with the sponsoring religious tradition. Being 'hostile' is a fourth stage that some may reach after appointment. The number of professing Catholics declines because of a more open approach to admissions and appointment of academic staff. The secular values of society replace the theological values of the Church. Chaplaincy provision focuses on therapy and counselling methods and becomes another 'service' to students. The institution no longer presumes religious commitments in its student body. Students are seen as free to make their own decisions and life choices, and no moral or religious considerations are accepted as part of the rules of the institution – the language of inclusion and pluralism are the new controls. Faith becomes a private matter, and religious symbols, or symbolism, are either removed, neglected, or understood differently. The demand is for academic excellence and inclusion within the secular educational mainstream, which means regarding the school or university's religious tradition as being reduced to extracurricular activities.

Conclusion

We have been discussing philosophies of education that are fundamentally negative in their teleology. They do not foster an openness to the presence of the transcendent truth. It is argued that we must reject the view that

Catholicism and radical secular philosophies of education are fundamentally compatible because they constitute a substantive set of philosophical commitments that are contrary to the basic beliefs of Catholicism. They are philosophical forces that act to neutralise Catholic education dissolving its theological aims. Sceptics within the Church often join with agnostics and atheists to pose objections to some forms of Catholic education based on their naturalistic and analytic philosophies. While the Church claims to reject nothing that is true in these philosophies, the incorporation into Catholic thinking of elements of these philosophies has redefined what Catholic education has become and created an amorphous philosophy of Catholic education. We need an emboldened response to these oppositional philosophies in education founded upon the existing resources of the Catholic tradition. Paddy Walsh (2018) rightly calls for 'a reasonably constructive and confident openness to opposing theories', but Catholic education cannot and should not presume that these secular philosophies can aid the mission of the Church. Scripture warns us against false idols, and yet ideologies are a form of idolatry which elevate their educational philosophies above God. Secularism is an ideology that worships the present age. It is why many educationalists now place the ascendency of their preferred ideologies ahead of any commitment to faith or reason (open inquiry).

Conclusion

This short book has argued that we live in an age when the reigning philosophical presuppositions are generally antagonistic to Catholicism. Within this frame, Catholic theories of education are multiple and are usually amalgams of different secular philosophies mixed with some religious views. Catholic education can certainly have a capacity for singularity and multiplicity based on the lived experience of diverse Catholics. The Church does not speak on Catholic education with an unequivocal and unambiguous voice. A plurality of educational positions has surfaced which do not simply differ but often conflict with each other. Even worse, the advocates of these positions align themselves with either the current Pope or his predecessors causing damage to the unity of the Church.

On one side of the debate, we see a focus on the social nature of human beings and less emphasis on Christian revelation or tradition. Tradition is seen as emphasising differences rather than similarities; it is seen as un-ecumenical, defensive, divisive, and even mere apologetics. On the traditionalist side, we see an emphasis on the dogmatic basis of Catholic education and this slant tends to reject an eclectic approach to the philosophy of Catholic education because it is difficult to define and is forever changing. We certainly need more and better Catholic thinking on education – but we above all need a more certain philosophy of Catholic education grounded in some sense of coherence. We ought not to Catholicise everything that the Catholic educationalist or philosopher write or say. In the same way, if an institution identifies as Catholic, or is identifiable as Catholic, it does not necessarily follow that they ought to be counted as Catholic because this may lead to blurred and fuzzy boundaries. The most basic function of Catholic education is to assist parents in educating their children in the faith.

A Vessel of Salvation

Sean Whittle (2015) in discussing the goals of Catholic education makes brief use of the metaphor of a ship requiring repairs while at sea in stormy waters.

Conclusion

The use of a ship in Christian symbolism has ancient origins and was a much-favoured image of the Church Fathers. In fact, the ship became the symbol of the Church and Hippolytus compared the Church to a boat tossed in the stormy ocean, 'The world is a sea in which the Church, like a ship, is beaten by the waves, but not submerged'. St Boniface echoes this when he said, 'In her voyage across the ocean of the world, the Church is like a great ship being pounded by the waves of life's different stresses. Our duty is not to abandon ship but to keep her on her course'. The analogy usually tells the story of the pilgrim Church as a ship, out on the turbulent high seas of disbelief and false philosophies (of education), in search of eternal life. This idea was given concrete form architecturally in Churches built prior to the 1960s which were often built with a nave, in Latin meaning 'ship' – read *nautilus*, and the ceilings over the nave were constructed with exposed wooden beams symbolising the reversed look of a ship's keel together with windows resembling portholes. The Christian belief is that the ship is indestructible because it is Peter's barque and therefore will not sink but will rather reach calmer waters in due course guided by the wooden mast in the form of a Cross and sails that are wind powered by the power of the Holy Spirit. Repairs to a ship will always be necessary, but we should remember that survival when we are all at sea is often based on unity of purpose (a clear telos) and the knowledge acquired from past seamanship (tradition). The symbolism can be much deeper theologically, and the bishop is often seen as the captain of the ship, with clergy as the crew, leading the congregation to distant shores on a voyage to salvation.

To use this ship analogy in discussing the purpose and philosophy of Catholic educational institutions requires that you first believe that these institutions are an integral part of the ecclesial mission of the Church and that they are organically part of the Church that serves its mission. Whittle's brief use of the ship analogy reminds me of the well-known thought experiment in philosophy called the *Ship of Theseus* which raises the question of whether an object that has all its components replaced is still fundamentally the same object. Plutarch in his *Life of Theseus* describes the paradox thus:

> The ship wherein Theseus and the youth of Athens returned from Crete had thirty oars, and was preserved by the Athenians down even to the time of Demetrius Phalereus, for they took away the old planks as they decayed, putting in new and stronger timber in their places, in so much that this ship became a standing example among the philosophers, for the logical question of things that grow; one side holding that the ship remained the same, and the other contending that it was not the same.

Clearly, the philosophers here debate the issue, some for and others against whether something is no longer what it proclaims to be. The Church should welcome a similar debate today about whether Catholic education is, after so much 'repair', essentially the same thing in time and place. For example, in science fiction, you will find characters who have their body parts replaced with modern artificial replacements until the person has been entirely replaced – if we compare this to some Catholic educational institutions, we can legitimately ask if they are still authentically Catholic.

Another famous analogy is the *Ship of Fools* found in Book 6 of Plato's *Republic*. There are parallels that can be made with some current forms of Catholic education. Plato's analogy speaks of a ship adrift at sea in uncertain waters with a 'short-sighted' captain who 'doesn't know much about navigation'. Since the leadership on board is directionless, the crew are consequently fighting with each other for control of the ship and view the navigator's role (the philosopher) on board as pointless and throw him overboard. The ship sails without direction and eventually runs aground because of the chaos that has ensued on board. It is helpful to unpack this analogy in relation to the state of Catholic education leadership and the lack of an overarching philosophy of Catholic education that would command endorsement and support from the Catholic Church.

First, I think there is more than one ship, but rather there are many different ships representing varied Catholic educational institutions all claiming the same identity, purpose, and destination – some are small rafts, others are kayaks or small fishing boats, while others are cruise ships, yachts, and perhaps even one or two aircraft carriers. Each vessel has a different crew and passengers, some welcome all on board (open admissions), and others may ask for some experience of seamanship (mainly Catholics). Second, the destination must be clear for all onboard these vessels, but some boats and ships have several compasses each representing different aims for their educational telos, and this causes confusion among the crew. Whoever oversees the helm must steer the vessel in line with the common telos, but there is disagreement among the crew on the direction to be taken. The interpretation and legitimacy of the teaching authority of the Church, scripture, tradition, and revelation are all debated endlessly. Some decide to row the boat themselves in new ways and directions abandoning how it was done previously. They are convinced they know best and have the knowledge to steer the ship in 'the right' direction, irrespective of what the passengers think. They begin to follow other ships with an alternative telos. Some are even content to stay in port to preserve the ship.

Third, the vessels sail through unpredictable waters that they appear to have little control over (the weather), but the stormy water represents the environment of different and sometimes hostile philosophies that seek to alter the course of the vessel. Some of these philosophies of education could be likened to sea monsters who cause damage to the structure of the vessel by using their tentacles to seep into the boat undetected, making it harder to steer and sail the vessel in the right direction. Secularism is such a monster in this regard as it is like the water monster Hydra with many heads, but if you cut one off, it would regrow two heads. The capacity of secularism to regenerate itself in the form of multiple philosophies of education is a danger because it is not always recognised how dangerous the implications of these philosophies are. From naturalism to atheism, they comprise the deadly components of secularism that dominate the Western worldview. We need to understand and see these philosophies coming from a distance and navigate a way around them because we cannot completely insulate ourselves from the dangers of the sea, but we may be able to deflect some of the hostile waves.

Fourth, the image of the captain here who is unable to steer the boat out of troubled waters and into more suitable environments can be a comment on the leadership of Catholic educational institutions by both clerical and lay leaders. Of course, there are many excellent captains of Catholic institutions navigating well despite the challenges. They know that the command of the vessel is vital for a successful voyage, and this requires the vessel to be well designed and maintained to ensure that it can sail to its destination despite the storms it will face. The captain needs to be on the bridge looking ahead to guide the ship on its journey watching out for and taking note of lighthouses (Church teaching on education) to avoid the rocks, reefs, or icebergs of false philosophies.

In order that the ship is shipshape, all the crew and passengers must be trained in their respective roles. All the sailors need some skills in navigation on board and know why and where they are heading – they need to prepare themselves and the passengers for their destination's end (salvation). Each vessel will face many obstacles and uncertainties (negative teleologies) on the journey and may have to change direction at times to avoid a dangerous storm but will find a way back to their original destination if they believe. False philosophies of education can hit a vessel hard either in the form of a major storm or iceberg but, as said already, more usually through seeping into the ship gradually without notice causing it to lose direction or forcing it to sail to another destination (secularism). It may even sink the ship or cause it to run aground like in Plato's analogy of the *Ship of Fools*. While the effects of secularism take effect, many of the crew are asleep, in denial, or ignorant about the danger facing them and focus their attention instead on rearranging the deck chairs, and while the passengers are also distracted, the ship is sinking. Their focus is not on the main thing but on the trivial.

Discussion about philosophies of Catholic education has not always been easy or respectful. Keeping with the ship analogy, some might see it like a naval battle, as St Basil the Great wrote in the aftermath of the Council of Nicaea in 325:

> To what shall I liken our present condition? It may be compared, I think, to some naval battle which has arisen out of time old quarrels and is fought by men who cherish a deadly hate against one another, of long experience in naval warfare, and eager for the fight.
>
> (quoted by Di Noia, 2021)

Basil gives a vivid description of disagreement after the Council where no consensus was immediately apparent, and some issues remained unresolved. Much could be said of different philosophies of Catholic education today that are in constant flux and disarray.

There is disagreement about their future direction, but even with the challenges to be faced, we should ask is some resolution necessary for an assured journey to the right port? Currently, there are ships that claim to be Catholic that are unmoored in any port and appear to be without an anchor to steady the ship because there is no singular definition of what it means, and it remains at sea unsettled and distant from its home (tradition) and is unable to find its true destination as there is no agreement by the sailors on which compass to use or an experienced and wise captain on board to steer the ship. Multiple routes through the ocean have become the accepted norm, but where they land eventually is uncertain. My use of the ship analogy here is not only to simply encourage and provoke thinking about exploring a philosophy of Catholic education but also perhaps to stem the tide of negative waves of incompatible philosophies.

Multiple challenges therefore face any attempt to outline a philosophy of Catholic education because not all these philosophies are consistent with Catholic formation. I have previously argued that Catholic education has become less and less distant from mainstream secular education because a unique philosophy of Catholic education does not exist or demonstrated in a substantive way in most Catholic educational institutions and is therefore rarely articulated (Arthur, 1995). Moreover, a high level of distinctiveness must be one of the features of Catholic identity, alongside the experience of a high sense of continuity with traditional Catholic culture. A sense of continuity can also be achieved by constructing strong commitments that provide certainty and direction in life. When we are dealing with Catholic education's philosophical underpinnings, we need a theological reference point. And we have it in Christ in his Church. Christ is the foundation of Catholic education, which teaches communion with Christ through the experience of prayer and the Church's liturgical and sacramental tradition. Catholic education ought to help students become Christ-like as it calls them to perfect humanity, as Christ was perfectly human. It must prepare the students to receive and grow in God's sanctifying grace. Catholic education also imparts a Christian vision of the world, of life, and of culture. Catholic education requires an all-round Christocentric education and formation. However, the reality is that profound changes in the Catholic Church have continued to encourage a less distinctive or traditional approach, and this is partly due to a minimal degree of continuity in the Catholic education tradition. Boeve (2005) believes that Catholic education is characterised today by detraditionalisation and pluralisation which leads to Catholic educational institutions, of all types, bearing little resemblance to their predecessors.

There was previously a Thomist philosophy of education providing direction and a reference point for education, but this has largely disappeared, and nothing has replaced it. There is rampant doubt and scepticism about almost everything which has encouraged different forms of relativism and a multiplicity of educational philosophies. The multiplicity of diverse facets and often diffuse philosophies of Catholic education, as operated by individual Catholic institutions, has in turn resulted in much celebration of change and ambiguity. The Vatican accepts and recognises multiple and competing perspectives in education, and because of this tolerance of ambiguity and the increasingly ill-defined nature of Catholic education, we have uncertainty, unpredictability, conflicting directions, multiple options, and unclear guidance which allows for the accommodation of apparent opposites and even legal disputes (see Arthur, 1994). As Cuypers (2004) observes,

> Among progressive Catholics in particular, there is a marked tendency to downgrade the distinctiveness of Catholic education, as if one should be ashamed to bear witness to the truths and values of one's own Catholic denomination. Aside from some hollow Christian slogans, Catholicism's identity becomes woolly and unfocused in progressive discourse. In an indiscriminate atmosphere of ecumenical and multicultural equality, the distinctiveness of Catholic education becomes blunted and ill-defined.

In the end, this leads to misunderstandings of the faith and anthropology, a pick-and-choose attitude to key elements of the faith and a broad ignorance of the faith itself. Schools, for many Catholics, are no longer seen as the context for nurturing the faith.

It is truly a fragmented realm with philosophical pluralism growing with increased diversity of perspectives. And yet the Christian message is that life is not fragmented or aimless. How therefore can this fragmentation be repaired? The idea of strengthening Catholic identity where such identity is varied, fluid, and fragmentary is inconclusive at best. While there is nothing new about fundamental disagreement in philosophy, we should acknowledge that there are oppositional philosophical perspectives that have gained some voice in Catholic education. There are two overlapping sites of disagreement: first, disagreements about what Catholic education is and how to practice it, and second, disagreements of a broadly interpretative kind about the meaning of aspects of Catholic education. Can there be a synthesis going forward? Currently, seeking consensus on different arguments for Catholic identity and any educational philosophy of Catholic education are potentially unbridgeable with the possibility of a resolution remote.

If the nature of Catholic education is such that we should not expect consensus, then it seems we should therefore not be troubled by that lack of consensus. However, we need to explore these disagreements and the multiplicity of perspectives because there is concern that philosophical positions, that is, generalised views of the world, could depart from the authentic characteristics of Catholic education. Witnessing to faith in the face of the plurality of Catholic education, while maintaining some degree of attachment to Catholic tradition, is vital. Can these different philosophies of education have a common core? Can this multiplicity have interrelated and interdependent elements? The diversity of Catholic expression in education, in perspectives, and even in convictions must has insuperable limits. Some of these limits are imposed in the Christian message found in Scripture while others by the teaching Church. There also needs to be recognisable patterns of practice between schools and universities that claim the title Catholic. Catholic schools and universities have a broader mission than a Catholic formation that enables all students to flourish, but it ought to be simultaneously forming lives of faith, love, and hope in the light of Jesus Christ.

Catholic education manifests itself differently in each country taking on different forms in time and place. Therefore, it is recognised that Catholic education cannot be properly understood in the abstract, independent of its actualisation in a particular societal context (see Haldane, 2023). While contextualisation is not the same as fragmentation, this leads to the question what makes a Catholic educational institution Catholic? Is it the crucifixes on the wall, the statues, or paintings of saints in the corridors, occasional Masses, and religious education classes, or is it something deeper? Is it the fact that, in institutional form, it is simply recognised by and under the jurisdiction of the local Catholic religious authorities? Catholic education is concerned with the mystery of being and its import for questions of our relationship to ourselves, the world and God. The common elements are that a philosophy/theology of Catholic education is (1) person-centred, (2) seeks the integral development of the person, (3) is a call to service, (4) promotes freedom, and (5) Christ is the model of an integrated fully human life, lived freely in the service of others. We need a full reassessment of a philosophical nature which will require a multi-disciplinary approach. At the heart of this is the question of the nature of the human being and the purpose and meaning of our lives.

We return to forging a modest link between the Neo-Scholastic legacy and current concerns in Catholic education. While secular philosophy of education was first seen as emerging as a way of learning from the John Dewey Society founded in 1935, we know that Catholic writing and understandings of philosophy of education were active at the end of the 19th century – more than 40 years earlier than secular alternatives. In contrast to these secular interpretations, it was already well known that Aquinas had an optimistic view of the possibilities of human intelligence. Thomas Joseph White (2011) has concluded,

> The classical philosophical heritage offers us a powerful resource. It has been tested by the fires of time, and its wisdom endures through the ages. If we engage with it intelligently, this tradition will cast intense light even

into the heart of our contemporary world, inviting it to turn away from the irrational shadows of secularism and toward the mystery of God.

Catholic educators largely want their institutions to remain Catholic, but they realise that being Catholic is not exactly what it was in the past. Those of a progressive mindset see the golden age in the future. Today, many of them promote a radical inclusion that aims to embrace everyone and as a result advocate a non-confessional Catholic education that largely abandons evangelisation and catechesis. In discerning the 'signs of the times' the danger is, as the French poet Charles Peguy wrote, modern Christians are people who do not believe what they believe. The teachings of Thomas Aquinas ought to become a reference point for any philosophy of Catholic education.

Teachers as well as students need to have an integral formation in the Catholic understanding of education. Any education course that forms teachers for teaching in Catholic schools needs to include a thorough introduction to the vision of the person represented by a Catholic anthropology (Roberts and O'Shea, 2022). Even if this course begins at the intellectual and theoretical level, it should ultimately be integrated in the practice of education. Catholic educational philosophy is as much about practice as it is about theory. That, at least, is a point of overlap between Catholic and Deweyan educational philosophies. Elias (1999) recommends that we focus on a Catholic theory of education rather than philosophy to accommodate the interdisciplinarity of the field and recognise the various viewpoints. One's religious identity consists of various elements and experiences, which make it unique. However, in the end, Catholic educational institutions ought to have an ecclesial mission to evangelise and catechise baptised Catholics through an integral education that furnishes a catholic identity and formation that when operationalised in society transforms culture. Catholicism is not a sect exclusively concerned about its own members and is therefore always inclusive of others. It seeks and wills the good of all or as Benedict XVI (2023: 18) describes it 'Catholic: the attribute of the Church ... reminds us that the Church of Jesus Christ has never been concerned with only one nation or only one culture, but that from the start it was destined for humanity'.

Every Catholic educational institution needs to meet minimal criteria to justify the title Catholic. Some of these criteria will be laid down in canon law, particularly the role of episcopal oversight of ecclesial entities. However, a theology and philosophy of Catholic education must express the institution's Christo-centric mission and identity. They will, as far as possible, synthesise different philosophical and theological accounts of Catholic education focusing on the similarities rather than on the differences. This undertaking should include and combine both contemporary and Neo-Scholastic understandings, not least serious reflections concerning the Catholic markers of evangelisation, re-evangelisation, pre-evangelisation, catechesis, identity formation, integral education, the common good, service, sacramental and prayer life,

Catholic anthropology and theology, and liberal education, all fusing with the mission of Catholic education. Generic expressions of this fusion should be avoided so that each institution can be held accountable through an agreed evaluation process.

Excellence in to the education provided must address the 'whole-student', and while the community to be formed is open to all, it ought not to compromise on its markers of Catholicism. It is through this lens of reaching consensus that a way forward might be possible along the lines being demonstrated by analytic Thomism which combines the methodology of analytic philosophy with themes of Thomas Aquinas and those who write on Thomism. The foundational core of Catholic education needs a coherent philosophy and the Christian anthropology that represents the core ought not to be reduced to the simple study of human behaviour. As John Haldane (2023) comments,

> It is also essential to appreciate, and to communicate to students, that in contrast to many contemporary views, which increasingly are forcing themselves upon the young, the Catholic understanding places all aspects of the human within a rich and expansive unitary vision. Far from being restrictive, this frees us from the pressures of reductive accounts whether of the highly sexualised, consumerist, materialistic or political sorts now current, and recovers an ennobling and inspirational vision of the human person.

References

Adler, M. J. (1984) *The Paideia Program: An Educational Syllabus*, New York: Macmillan.
Apple, M. (1979) *Ideology and Curriculum*, London: Routledge and Kegan Paul.
Arendt, H. (1954) The Crisis in Education, in *Between Past and Future*, New York, Viking Press.
Arthur, J. (1994) The Ambiguities of Catholic Schooling, *Westminster Studies in Education*, 17: 1, 65–77.
Arthur, J. (1995) *The Ebbing Tide: Policy and Principles of Catholic Education*, Leominster: Gracewing.
Arthur, J. (2009) Secularisation, Secularism, and Catholic Education: Understanding the Challenges, *International Studies in Catholic Education*, 1: 2, 228–239.
Arthur, J. (2013) The De-Catholisation of the Curriculum in English Catholic Schools, *International Studies in Catholic Education*, 5: 1, 83–98.
Arthur, J. (2021) *A Christian Education in the Virtues: Character Formation and Human Flourishing*, London: Routledge. See also Arthur, J. (2020) *The Formation of Character in Education: From Aristotle to the 21st Century*, London: Routledge.
Arthur, J., Kristjánsson, K. and Vogler, C. (2021) Seeking the Common Good in Education Through a Positive Conception of Social Justice, *British Journal of Educational Studies*, 69: 1, 101–117.
Arthur, J. and Nicholls, G. (2007) *John Henry Newman*, London: Continuum.
Balthasar, H. U. (1985) *A Short Primer for Unsettled Laymen*, San Francisco: Ignatius Press.
Benedict, XVI (2023) *What Is Christianity: The Last Writings*, San Francisco: Ignatius Press.
Bergman, R. (2011) *Catholic Social Learning: Educating the Faith That Does Justice*, New York: Fordham University Press.
Boatens, J. D. (2019) *Catholic Education: Mission and Challenges*, Christian Faith Publishing.
Boeve, L. (2005) Religion after Detraditionalization: Christian Faith in a Post-Secular Europe, *Irish Theological Quarterly*, 70: 99–122.
Boland, V. (2012) St Thomas Aquinas: What Is His Relevance to Catholic Education Today, *International Studies in Catholic Education*, 4: 2, 122–135.
Boys, M. C. (1989) *Educating in Faith: Maps and Visions*, California: Harper and Row.
Broudy, H. S. (1961) *Building a Philosophy of Education*, New Jersey: Prentice Hall.
Bryk, A., Lee, V. and Holland, P. (1995) *Catholic Schools and the Common Good*, Cambridge: Harvard University Press.

References

Butler, J. D. (1966) *Idealism and Education*, New York: Harper Row.
Casson, A. (2014) Fragmented Catholicity and Social Cohesion: Faith Schools in a Plural Society, Review by Madero, C., in *Journal of Catholic Education*, 18: 1, 201–203.
Chesterton, J. K. (1950) A New Case for Catholic Schools, in Chesterton, J. K., *The Common Man*, London: Sheed and Ward.
Comensoli, P. (2019) Schooling Catholic – A Presentation to the Leadership of Catholic Schools, Archdiocese of Melbourne.
Congregation for Catholic Education (CCE), The Catholic School, Vatican, 1977.
Curren, C. E. (1997) The Catholic Identity of Catholic Institutions, *Theological Studies*, 58: 90–108.
Cuypers, S. E. (2004) The Ideal of a Catholic Education in a Secularized Society, *Journal of Catholic Education*, 7: 4, 426–445.
De Lubac, H. (1995) *The Drama of Atheist Humanism*, San Francisco: Ignatius Press.
Dearden, R. F. (1982) Philosophy of Education, 1952–1982, *British Journal of Educational Studies*, 30: 1, 57–71.
Delfra, L. A. *et al* (2018) Education in a Catholic Key, in Jeynes, W. H., *The Wiley Handbook of Christian Education*, New Jersey: Wiley-Blackwell.
Dennick, R. (2012) Twelve Tips for Incorporating Educational Theory into Teaching Practices, *Medical Teaching*, 34: 618–624.
Diez de Rio, I. (2016) 'Postmodernidad y Nueva Religiosidad', *Religion and Culture*, 39, 55–91.
Di Noia, J. A. (2021) The Teaching of the Second Vatican Council in Current Catholic Theology, *The Thomist*, 85: 1, 127–138.
Donlon, T. C. (1952) *Theology of Education*, Dubuque: William Brown Company.
D'Souza, M.O. (1996) The Preparation of Teachers for Roman Catholic Schools: Some Philosophical First Principles, *Philosophical Inquiry in Education*, 9: 2, 1–16.
D'Souza, M. O. (2016) *A Catholic Philosophy of Education: The Church and Two Philosophers*, Montreal: McGill-Queens University Press.
Elias, J. L. (1995) *Philosophy of Education: Classical and Contemporary*, Malabar, Florida: Krieger Publishing Company.
Elias, J. L. (1999) Whatever Happened to Catholic Philosophy of Education, *Religious Education*, 94: 1, 92–110.
Elias, J. L. and Nolan, L. (2009) *Educators in the Catholic Intellectual Tradition*, Fairfield, Connecticut: Sacred Heart University Press.
Ellis, J. A. (2001) A Philosophy of Catholic Education, in Hunt, T. C, Ellis, A. J. and Nuzzi, R. J. (eds.) *Handbook of Research on Catholic Education*, Westport, Connecticut: Greenwood Press.
Feuer, L. S. (2010) *Ideology and the Ideologists*, London: Transaction Publications.
Fitzpatrick, E. A. (1953) *A Philosophy of Education*, Milwaukee: Bruce Publishing.
Fitzpatrick, E. A. (1954) The Catholic College of the Future, *Catholic School Journal*, 55: 128.
Franchi, L. (2016) Being Open to Others in Catholic Schools, *International Journal of Catholic Education*, 2.
Franchi. L. (2023a) Editorial: Catholic Education and the Liberal Arts, *Religions*, 14: 539–542.
Franchi, L. (2023b) *Thomas Shields and the Renewal of Catholic Education*, Washington DC: Catholic University of America Press.
Francis, P. (2020) *The Global Compact*, Vatican City.

References

Gallagher, T. (2004) Education in Divided Societies, Basingstoke: Palgrave Macmillan

Garcia-Huidobro, J. C. (2017) What Are Catholic Schools Teaching to Make a Difference, *Journal of Catholic Education*, 20: 2, 64–95.

Geusau, C. A. and Booth, P. (2013) *Catholic Education in the West: Roots, Reality and Revival*, Grand Rapids: Acton Institute.

Gilson, E. (1948) *History of Philosophy and Philosophical Education*, Milwaukee: Marquette University Press.

Groome, T. (2021) *What Makes Catholic Education Catholic*, New York: Orbis Books.

Groppo, G. (1991) *Teologia dell'educazione: Origine, Identitá, Compiti*, Rome, Libreria: Ateneo Salesiano.

Gulley, A. D. (1965) *The Educational Philosophy of Saint Thomas Aquinas*, New York: Pageant Press.

Gutek, G. L. (1997) *Philosophical and Ideological Perspectives on Education*, Boston: Allyn and Bacon.

Haack, R. J. (1976) Philosophies of Education, *Philosophy*, 51: 196, 159–176.

Habermas, J. (2003) Faith and Knowledge, in Jürgen Habermas, *The Future of Human Nature*, trans. by Beister, H., Pensky, M. and Rehg W., Cambridge: Polity Press. See also Habermas, J. and Ratzinger, J. (2007) *The Dialectics of Secularization*, San Francisco: Ignatius Press.

Haldane, J. (2004) *Faithful Reason: Essays Catholic and Philosophical*, London: Routledge.

Haldane, J. (2023) Understanding the Human Person – The Catholic Perspective, Archdiocese of Melbourne.

Hamm, C. M. (1989) *Philosophical Issues in Education: An Introduction*, London: Routledge.

Hancock, C. L. (2017) *Recovering a Catholic Philosophy of Elementary Education*, Redpath, Pennsylvania: Newham House Press.

Hauerwas, S. (2007) The State of the University, Oxford: Blackwell.

Hirst, P. (1974) *Moral Education in a Secular Society*, London: London University Press.

Holder, A. G. (1992) Saint Basil the Great on Secular Education and Christian Virtue, *Religious Education*, 87: 3, 395–415.

Hunt, T. C., Ellis, A. J. and Nuzzi, R. J. (2001) (eds.) *Handbook of Research on Catholic Education*, Westport, Connecticut: Greenwood Press.

Jordan, E. B. (1931) *The Philosophy of Catholic Education*, New York: Benziger Brothers.

Kelty, B. J. (1999) Towards a Theology of Catholic Education, *Religious Education*, 94: 1, 5–23.

MacIntyre, A. (1971) *Against the Self-Images of the Age: Essays on Ideology and Philosophy*, London: Gerald Duckworth.

Madero, C. (2015) Theological Dynamics of Paulo Freire's Educational Theory, *International Studies in Catholic Education*, 7:2.

Maritain, J. (1943) *Education at the Crossroads*, New Haven: Yale University Press.

Maritain, J. (1962) *An Introduction to Philosophy*, New York: Sheed and Ward.

Maritain, J. (1996) *Integral Humanism*, Illinois: Notre Dame University Press.

McCluskey, N. G. (1959) *Catholic Viewpoint on Education*, Chicago: Loyola University Press.

McCool, G. A. (2000, 1995) *The Neo-Thomist*, Milwaukee: Marquette University Press.

References

McCool, G. A. (2000, 1995) The Ideal of the Catholic Mind, in Cernera, A. J. (ed.), *Continuity and Plurality and Catholic Theology*, Fairfield, Connecticut: Sacred Heart University Press.

McDonough, G. P. (2012) *Beyond Obedience and Abandonment: Toward a Theory of Dissent in Catholic Education*, Montreal: McGill Queens University Press.

McDonough, G. P. (2016) Cultivating Identities: The Catholic School as Diverse Ecclesial Space, *Philosophical Inquiry in Education*, 23: 2, 160–177.

McGucken, W. J. (1943, 1950, 1954) *The Philosophy of Catholic Education*, New York: American Press.

McGucken, W. J. and Sheridan, M. P. (1966) *Catholic Philosophy of Education*, New York: America Press.

McLaughlin, T. H. (2002) A Catholic Perspective on Education, *International Journal of Christianity and Education*, 6: 2, 121–134.

McLaughlin, T. H., O'Keefe, J. and O'Keefe, B. (1996) *The Contemporary Catholic School: Context, Identity and Diversity*, London: The Falmer Press.

Meyer, M. H. (1929) *The Philosophy of Teaching of St Thomas Aquinas*, Milwaukee: Bruce Publishing.

Miller, M. J. (2006) *The Holy See's Teaching on Catholic Schools*, Atlanta: Sophia Institute Press.

Morley, M. M. and Piderit, J. J. (2006) *Catholic Higher Education*, Oxford: Oxford University Press.

Newman, J. H. (1982) *The Idea of a University*, Ilinois: University of Notre Dame Press.

O'Donnell, C. L. (1930) *The Philosophy of Catholic Education*, Washington DC: National Council of Catholic Men.

O'Malley, J. (2008) *Whatever Happened to Vatican II*, Cambridge: Harvard University Press.

Ornstein, A. C. and Levine, D. U. (2003) *Foundations of Education* (8th ed.), Boston: Houghton-Mifflin.

Ozmon, H. and Craver, S. M. (2003) *Philosophical Foundations of Education* (7th ed.), New Jersey: Merrill Prentice Hall.

John Paul II. (1998) *Fides Et Ratio*, Vatican City.

Peters, R. S. (1966) *Ethics and Education*, London: George Allen and Unwin.

Piderit, J. J. and Morley, M. M. (2012) *Teaching the Tradition: Catholic Themes in Academic Disciplines*, Oxford: Oxford University Press.

Pollefeyt, D. (2023) *Review of the Religious Education Curriculum for Catholic Schools in the Archdiocese of Melbourne*, Belgium: University of Leuven.

Pring, R. (1968) Has Education an Aim? in Tucker, B. (ed.) *Catholic Education in a Secular Society*, London: Sheed and Ward.

Pring, R. (2018) *The Future of Publicly Funded Faith Schools: A Critical Perspective*, London: Routledge.

Redden, J. R. and Ryan, F. A. (1942) *A Catholic Philosophy of Education*, Wisconsin: Bruce Publishing.

Redpath, P. A. (2017) Preface, in Hancock, C. L. (ed.) *Recovering a Catholic Philosophy of Elementary Education*, Pennsylvania: Newham House Press.

Richards, M. (2019) *Faith in Dialogue: Recontextualising Catholic School Identity and Mission in a Diverse and Changing US*, PhD, *University of Leuven*.

Rist, J. and Rist, A. (2022) *Confusion in the West: Retrieving Traditions in the Modern and Post-Modern World*, Cambridge: Cambridge University Press.

Roberts, A. E. and O'Shea, G. (2022) The Integral Formation of Catholic Teachers, *Religions*, 13: 12, 1230.

Scanlan, M. (2008) The Grammar of Catholic Schooling and Radically 'Catholic' School, *Catholic Education: A Journal of Inquiry and Practice*, 12: 1, 24–54.

Schall, J. V. (2008) *The Mind That Is Catholic: Philosophical and Political Essays*, Washington DC: Catholic University of America Press.

Searle, J. R. (1996) The Case for a Traditional Liberal Education, *Journal of Blacks in Higher Education*, Autumn, 91–98.

Second Vatican Council. Declaration on Christian Education, 1965.

Shields T. E. (1917) Philosophy of Education, Washington DC: Catholic Education Press.

Strain, J. P. (1975) Idealism: A Clarification of an Educational Philosophy, *Educational Theory*, 25: 3, 263–271.

Sullivan, J. W. (2001) *Catholic Education: Distinctive and Inclusive*, Boston: Kluwer Academic.

Taylor, C. (2008) *A Secular Age*, Cambridge: Harvard University Press.

Topping, N. S. (2015) *Renewing the Mind: A Reader in the Philosophy of Catholic Education*, Washington DC: Catholic University of America.

Van Beeck, F. J. (1985) *Catholic Identity After Vatican II: 3 Types of Faith in One Church*, Chicago: Loyola University Press.

Vanderberg, D. (1983) *Being and Education: An Essay on Existential Phenomenology*, New Jersey: Prentice Hall.

Vincelette, A. (2011) *Recent Catholic Philosophy: The Twentieth Century*, Milwaukee: Marquette University Press.

Walsh, P. (2018) From Philosophy to Theology of Catholic Education, With Bernard Lonergan and Karl Rahner, *International Studies in Catholic Education*, 10: 2, 132–155.

White, T. J. (2011) Whether Faith Needs Philosophy, *First Things*, July.

Whittle, S. (2014) Towards a Contemporary Philosophy of Catholic Education: Moving the Debate Forward, *International Studies in Catholic Education*, 6: 1 46–59.

Whittle, S. (2015) *A Theory of Catholic Education*, London: Bloomsbury.

Whittle, S. (2017) *Vatican II and New Thinking About Catholic Education*, London: Routledge.

Wilson, J. (1979) *Preface to Philosophy of Education*, London: Routledge and Kegan Paul.

Woden, Q. (2019) Catholic Schools in Latin America and the Caribbean, *Estudios Sobre Educacion*, 37: 91–111.

Woods, T. E. (2008) *The Church Confronts Modernity: Catholic Intellectuals and the Progressive Era*, New York: Columbia University Press.

Wright, D. (2021) Etienne Gilson and the 'Christian Philosophy' of St Thomas Aquinas, *Academia, Letters*.

Wulf, C., (2002) Anthropology and Education, in Kopping, K. P. (ed.) *History of Theory of Anthropology*, Hamburg, Transaction Publications.

Zukowski, A. A. (2013) New Learning Paradigms for Catholic Education, *Journal of Catholic Education*, 1: 1, 51–66.

Index

Abelard, P. 25
Aeternis Patris 59–63
Albert the Great 56
analytical philosophy 5–6, 12, 74
Anonymous Christianity 46
Anscombe, G. E. M. 25
anti-Catholicism 60, 62
anti-racist theory 71
Aquinas, T. 11, 23, 25, 55–59, 64, 69, 91, 93
Arendt, H. 67
Aristotelianism 67
Aristotelian-Thomist philosophy 63, 65
Aristotle 11, 22–24, 56, 64
atican Dicastery for Education and Culture 45
Augustine 11, 24–25, 69–70

backwardism 14
Balthasar, H. U. 11
Baptised Catholic 37
Benedict, Pope 72
Benedictine 33
Bernard of Clairvaux 69
Bildung movement 40
Blondel, J.-F. 25
Boeve, L. 89
Boland, V. 64
Boys, M. 26
Breaking the Spell (Dennett) 70
Brighouse, H. 13
Broudy, H. S. 66
Bryk, A. 49
Bryk, B. 47
Butler, J. D. 66

Campbell, M. 14–15
cancel culture 41

capitalism 75
Carr, D. 12
Casson, A. 36
catechesis 4, 32, 35–38
Catechumenate 23
Catholic anthropology 21, 80
Catholic Atheist 37
Catholic Church 3, 6, 14, 42
Catholic consciousness 2
Catholic Dialogue School 80
Catholic education 7, 32, 61, 64, 66–69, 71, 85–92; in academic discourse 8; institutional sense of education 2; Marxism 76–77; models of 44–47; name-only 81–83; overview 1–2; philosophy of 1–4, 7, 10, 35, 67, 92; postmodernism 77–78; principles 3; purpose 5; radical implications 78–81; secularising philosophies of education 69–72; truth about human person 21; *see also* Thomism in education
Catholic Education in a Secular Society (Tucker) 5
Catholic educators 21
Catholic identity 6, 13, 44; in education 16–17; notion of 17
Catholic institutions 88; diversity 45
Catholic integral education 41
Catholicism 12, 66, 92
Catholicity 37, 50–51
Catholic liberal education 39–40
Catholic philosophers 10
Catholic Philosophy of Education, A 14
Catholic Philosophy of Education: The Church and Two Philosophers, A (D'Souza) 61
Catholic Pilgrim 37

Index

Catholic school 53
Catholic Schools and the Common Good 51
Catholic Schools on the Threshold of the Third Millennium 28
Chesterton, G. K. 19, 25
child abuse 70
Christian anthropology 50
Christian Apologetics 74
Christian evangelisation 7
Christian existentialism 66, 68
Christian symbolism 87
Christian virtue formation 39
Christo-centric mission 92
Christ's revelation 6
Church-cantered theology 34
Clemens, T. F. 23
Clement of Alexandria 23, 25
cohort goal 45
Col 2:8 23
Comenius, J. 11
Comensoli, P. 8
'common good' model 47–52
competition 13
congregation for Catholic Education 15–16; documents of 62; resources and guidance statements 16; *see also* Catholic education
consumption 13
Council of Nicaea 88
Crisis of Education, The 67
cultural Christian 36
Cuypers, S. E. 90

Dearden, R. F. 19
Declaration on Christian Education 1965 16, 28
degrees of secularity 72
Delfra, L. A. 43
de Lubac, H. 72
De Magistro (Aquinas) 60
De Maistre, J. 25
Dennett, D. C. 70
Descartes, R. 25
Dewey, J. 11–12, 59, 71
dialogue 17–18
diaspora goal 45
Dicastery for Education and Culture 14
Dicastery for Promoting Integral Human Development 41
dogmatic Catholicism 4
Dominican 33
Donlon, T. C. 19, 61

D'Souza, M. 47–48, 61
dualism 70
dualistic Catholic schools 46
dualistic model 45
Dun Scotus 25

Ebbing Tide, The 51
Educating to Intercultural Dialogue in Catholic School: Living in Harmony for a Civilisation of Love 42
educational philosophy 12, 24
educational theory and practice 9
Education and Experience (Dewey) 71
egoism 68
Elias, J. 61, 64–65, 91
Emile (Rousseau) 11
End of Faith, The (Harris) 70
Erasmus, D. 25
Ethics and Education (Peters) 12
evangelisation 4, 7, 32, 35
exclusivism 7
existentialism 68

Family Catholic 37
Feuer, L. S. 72
Fitzpatrick, E. 60
five Cs (Conscience, Competence, Compassion, Commitment, and Character) 34
fluidly faithful to Catholicism 4
formation in virtue 38
Francis, Pope 13–14, 17, 35
Franciscan 33
Freire, P. 77
Frenchmen, C. 19
Future of Publicly Funded Faith Schools: A Critical Perspective, The 6

Gall, J. 11
Gallagher, T. 46
Garcia-Huidobro, J. C. 46
gay and lesbian philosophy 71
Gen: 1:26 20; 1: 31 20
ghetto mentality 10
Gilson, E. 19
Global Compact for Education 13–14
global educational pact 43
God Delusion, The (Dawkins) 70
God Is Not Great (Hitchens) 70
Golden Rule Catholic 37
Gospel Values 22

Index

Gravissimum Educationis 28
Groome, T 28
Groppo, G. 28

Habermas, J. 75
Haldane, J. 93
Halfway Catholic 37
Hancock, C. L. 2, 21, 61
hardcore Catholic 37
Harris, S. 70
Hauerwas, S. 75
Hirst, P. 4
Holder, A. G. 74
holistic model 45
Holland, P. 47, 49
Holy Communion 28
Holy Spirit 32, 86
human awakening 57
human being 22, 57
human capital 38
human community in education 13
human intelligence 91
Humanism 67
human potentialities 5
hyper-liberalism 73

idealism 66–67, 72
identity 32, 35–38
Identity of the Catholic School for a Culture of Dialogue, The 16
immersion goal 45
individualism 13
indoctrination 6
Institute for Catholic Liberal Education (ICLE) 39–40
integral education 35, 38–42
integral humanism 41
I Pet 3:15 23
'ism' movements 5

Jardine, G. 11
Jesuit 33–34
Jesuit Catholic philosophy of education 34
John Dewey Society 91
Judeo-Christian heritage 41

Kelty, B. J. 28
Kreeft, P. 25

Lasallian 34
Lee, V. 47
Leo XIII, Pope 59

Letter to a Christian Nation 70
Lewis, C. S. 23, 74
liberal education 39–41, 68
liberal formation 35, 38–42
Life of Theseus 86
literature on Catholic education: dialogical 46; identity-focused 46; open 46; secular 46
Locke, J. 11, 59
Lonergan, B. 25
lumen gentium 1

MacIntyre, A. 23, 25
Magisterium 81
Maritain, J. 19, 24–25, 41, 64
Martyr, J. 69
Marxism 75–77
materialism 75
Matthew's Gospel 35
McCool, G. 61–62
McDonough, G. P. 78–81
McGucken, Fr. 40
McLaughlin, T. H. 14, 19, 25
mental freedom 7
meritocracy 75
Metaphysics (Aristotle) 56
Meyer, M. H. 59
Miller, M. 51
mission 32, 35
mission of Christ 14
Monique, P. 60
morality 78
Morley, M. M. 45
Muggeridge, M. 74

naturalism in education 11
neo-Scholasticism 59, 67
Neo-Thomism 7, 61
Newman, J. H. 25, 40–41, 69–70

O'Malley, J. 71
Outlines of Philosophical Education (Jardine) 11

Pascal, B. 25
Paul II, John 27, 65
Peguy, C. 91
perennialism 66
perennial philosophy 67
persuasion goal 45
Peters, R. S. 5, 12–13, 19
philosophical materialism 75
philosophical pluralism 27

philosophies of Catholic education 7, 9–17; anthropology and theology 20–27; 'Catholic' about 27–30; Catholic identity 17; 'closed' position 10; contemporary 10; continuum 10; dialogue 17–18; discipline 9; diversity 27; 'open' position 10; overview 9; partial philosophies 18–20; *see also* Catholic education
Philosophy of Education (Tate) 11
Philosophy of Education: Classical and Contemporary (Elias) 61
Philosophy of Teaching of St. Thomas Aquinas, The 60
Piderit, J. J. 45
Pius XI, Pope 59
Plato 11, 24, 87–88
Platonism 67
Pollefeyt, D. 80
polyphony of movements 14, 42–44
Pope Paul VI 32
postmodernism 76–78
postmodernity 70
post-Vatican II Roman Catholicism 26
Practical Enquiry into a Philosophy of Education, A (Gall) 11
pre-evangelisation 4
Pring, R. 5–6
progressive elements of education 69
Progressive Zeitgeist 66
progressivism 67
Purnell S. J., P. 81

Rahner, K. 46
realism 58, 66, 72
reconfessionalisation of Catholic schools 80
Recovering a Catholic Philosophy of Elementary Education (Hancock) 61
Redden, J. R. 14
Redpath, P. A. 18
re-evangelisation 4
Reid, L. A. 12
religious charisms 32; education 32–33
religious orders or communities 33; Benedictine 33; Dominican 33; Franciscan 33; Jesuit 33–34; Lasallian 34; Salesian 34
Renaissance humanists 27
Republic (Plato) 87
Resurrection of Jesus Christ 22

Rio, Diez de 78
Rousseau, J.-J. 11
Ryan, F. A. 14

Salesian 34
Salvation 85–93
Scanlan, M. 49
Schall, J. 7
scholastic realism 59
School Catholic 37
scripture 22
Searle, J. R. 78
sectarianism 6
secular education 73
secularism 70, 74–75, 87–88
self-activity 58
selfishness 68
Shields, T. 59
ship analogy 87–89
Ship of Fools 87–88
Ship of Theseus 86
social character of the human person 49
sociologism 18
socio-political philosophies 74
Spalding, J. 61
spirit of criticism 5
spiritual formation 38
St. Ambrose Centre for Catholic Liberal Education and Culture 40
St Basil of Caesarea 74
St. Benedict 25
St. Bernard of Clairvaux 25
St Boniface 86
St Ignatius of Loyola 25
Strain, J. P. 66
subjective self 11
Summa Contra Gentiles (Aquinas) 55
Summa Theologiae (Aquinas) 55–56
surrendering to the secular 10

Tate, T. 11
Taylor, C. 74
theistic philosophy of education 28–29
Theology of Education (Donlon). 19, 61
theoretical eclecticism 9
Thomism in education 7, 32, 55–59, 64, 72, 90; *Aeternis Patris,* response to 59–63; implications 63–64; revival of 67; *see also* Aquinas, T.
Thomism in Education (McCool) 61
transformative intellectual 75
Tucker, B. 5

values that Catholic educational institutions 22–23
Van Beeck, F. J. 37
Vanderberg, D. 66
Vatican II's *Declaration on Christian Education* 51
Vatican's Congregation for Catholic Education 15
Vincelette, A. 68

Walsh, P. 54, 84
Whatever Happened at Vatican II (O'Malley) 71

What Makes Catholic Education Catholic (Groome) 28
White, J. 12, 91
Whittle, S. 4, 25, 85
William of Ockham 25
Wilson, J. 4
Wollstonecraft, M. 11
Woods, T. 66
Wulf, C. 20

Zeitgeist 66

For Product Safety Concerns and Information please contact our EU representative GPSR@taylorandfrancis.com
Taylor & Francis Verlag GmbH, Kaufingerstraße 24, 80331 München, Germany

www.ingramcontent.com/pod-product-compliance
Lightning Source LLC
Chambersburg PA
CBHW071513150426
43191CB00009B/1506